Classic Restaurants

OF

DURHAM

Classic Restaurants

OF

DURHAM

CHRIS HOLADAY & PATRICK CULLOM

Foreword by Don Ball

AMERICAN PALATE

Published by American Palate
A Division of The History Press
Charleston, SC
www.historypress.com

First published 2020

Manufactured in the United States

ISBN 9781467143950

Library of Congress Control Number: 2019954237

Contents

Foreword

When my family moved to northern Durham in 1979, let's just say there wasn't much of a food scene there. This was long before the age of "foodies" and the internet, and reputations were made (and lost) by what you read in the newspaper or what you heard from your neighbors and friends. It was a word-of-mouth world that I was introduced to in the Bull City: on prom nights, young couples would go to the Saddle and Fox for a "fancy" date; families would flock to Hartman's Steak House to celebrate birthdays and anniversaries; Honey's, the diner on the interstate, was just about the only choice for food after 10:00 p.m. During our shift meals at Erwin Cotton Mill, my coworkers introduced me to Bullock's combination plate of barbecue and Brunswick stew; many of the cigarette factory workers at Liggett & Myers and American Tobacco shared a similar routine on the other side of downtown at Dillard's. And by the way, if you weren't in Durham back then and you want to get a taste of what food culture was like, just do an internet search for "At Home with Peggy Mann," and you'll see exactly what I'm talking about. Mann—who lived out by the Eno River on Cole Mill Road—hosted one of the first televised food shows from North Carolina. Everyone in Durham would watch it and be entertained—and educated.

Yes, Durham was still very much that kind of small town. We had a few niche restaurants with Chinese and Italian fare, but we'd travel to Chapel Hill and Raleigh if we wanted something new or trendy. Never in a million years would anyone have expected Durham's food scene to undergo such a beautiful transformation over the course of two generations. There were a lot of things that contributed to that change, and Chris and Patrick have done a wonderful job of documenting Durham's food history inside these pages. The restaurant industry is a fickle business that involves passion, a thick skin and a fluid checkbook. I speak from experience; I began my Durham food career as a Filet-O-Fish fry cook at the McDonald's on North Roxboro Road. I later became a bartender, because the evening hours and the lifestyle suited me. I got my first experience at Manella's, since my mom made desserts there (high praise for nepotism). There, they served the most amazing food in a cinder block room with the motto: "Our cuisine is our décor." I also made cocktails at the four-star Sheraton (now the Millennium) Hotel for patients of the rice diet. I once had a job pouring beer at Devine's, and one night, while I was working my shift, I was fired because I was sitting at the bar in Anotherthyme during my break. My favorite job, however, was shaking margaritas at Papagayo—the first Mexican restaurant in Durham—where I worked my way up to the managing position, and I eventually became the owner for eight years. By "owner," I mean I was hosting, cooking, washing dishes, slinging drinks, waiting tables and, in my free time, paying the bills, juggling the needs and responsibilities just like every other restaurant owner. But the relationships I forged there allowed me to eventually land what I have long said is the best food and beverage job in the state at the Washington Duke Inn. At the WaDu, I have worked beside hundreds of talented hospitality professionals and served—quite literally—hundreds of thousands of guests. I have been fortunate enough to grow with the property, and twenty-three years later, I'm still evolving. Times have changed; food has changed; people's palates and expectations have changed; and Durham has changed.

I can now walk to more than one hundred restaurants from my bungalow in Trinity Park. Yes, there's barbecue and burgers, pizza and pasta, but there's also Ethiopian, Peruvian, paninis, tempura, ramen, tapas, izakaya, ice cream, donuts and, yes, even southern fare. And get this—folks in Chapel Hill and Raleigh (and from far beyond) travel to Durham to eat their way through what is arguably the best food selection in the state of North Carolina. I wax nostalgic as I savor this delicious compilation of Durham's restaurant roots, and I actually begin to drool as I think back to some of my favorite plates and old haunts. I also chuckle as I am reminded of the life experiences and colorful cast of owners, servers, cooks and dishwashers that I met at all of Durham's extraordinary venues. But we'll save those stories for another time over a shared dinner.

—Don Ball

Since 1997, Don Ball has been the "king's taster" at Washington Duke Inn & Golf Club. He currently serves as the area director of operations at both the Washington Duke and JB Duke Hotels. In his free time, Don likes to bike and hike enough so he can eat good Durham food with abandon.

Acknowledgements

We would like to start by thanking the many people who shared their memories of Durham restaurants and assisted our research. Many thanks go to Bob Anthony, curator of the North Carolina Collection at the Wilson Special Collections Library at the University of North Carolina at Chapel Hill (UNC–Chapel Hill), as well as the archival processors and staff at the Digital Production Center for making Wilson Library's unique collections accessible and available for our research. The *Durham Herald* Photograph Collection was also immensely helpful. Housed in Wilson Library at UNC–Chapel Hill, the collection contains over 2 million images taken between 1945 and 2002. It is an invaluable resource for anyone interested in the history of Durham. Wilson Library at UNC–Chapel Hill is also home to the North Carolina Digital Heritage Center. This organization digitizes and publishes numerous historic materials, including city directories, online (digitalnc.org). These guides, which list businesses and employees from as far back as the late 1800s, were extremely helpful in tracing Durham's restaurant history. Additionally, we would like to thank Barbara Ilie and Elizabeth Shulman from the North Carolina Collection at the Durham County Library for their assistance with this project. Andre Vann, noted Durham historian and the archivist at North Carolina Central University, also provided us with valuable information and research assistance. We would also like to thank the Open Durham website; it is an invaluable resource for anyone interested in the history of the city.

Durham is a city built by tobacco. This 1940 view shows the American Tobacco complex just south of downtown. *Photo by Arthur Rothstein.Courtesy of the Library of Congress.*

Special thanks go to Don Ball, who shared memories from the many years he has spent involved with Durham restaurants in his foreword. Others who shared their memories and photos with us are Mel Melton, Josh Wittman, Gary Kueber, Wilma Dillard, Mike Howell, Ricky Moore, Michelle Cobb, Josh Bousel, Christa Slaughter, Chris Sutch, Lance Sawyers, Kim Walsh, Chris Reid, Rachel Hawkins, John Boy, Mike Martin, Amish and Shetal Desai, Wanda Walton, Bob Burtman, Belinda Rasmussen, Dawn Robson and Mike Knowles. We would also like to thank Kate Jenkins, our editor at The History Press, for her guidance and patience.

Patrick would like to thank his wonderful wife, Bonny, for her encouragement throughout this project and for listening to him talk (sometimes at length) about the restaurants and the photographers who photographed them. Chris would like to thank his wife, Sue, for exploring countless Durham restaurants with him over the past twenty-five years.

Introduction

More than any other type of business, restaurants are famous for pulling disappearing acts. They open—sometimes to great fanfare—and then are suddenly gone, often without warning. The restaurant business is tough, and every proprietor will tell you that it's all about finding that perfect combination of menu, location, price and service. Success in the restaurant business is also about fitting in to the community, and many restaurants that appear to have the recipe for success will still fail because they cannot find their niche. Despite the many challenges of the restaurant business, some do succeed. Every city has a handful of longtime dining establishments, and it is often at one of them that some of the locals' most indelible and cherished memories are formed. From birthdays and graduations, prom nights and first dates to countess other celebrations, these favorite restaurants often serve as the venue for important events. In the city of Durham, North Carolina, this tradition is no different.

The restaurant history of Durham is actually rather unique due to the city's distinct components. Durham began as nothing more than a country train depot; but eventually, in 1869, a community sprung up around the depot and was incorporated and named for the doctor who had initially donated the land for the depot. It was the area's popular tobacco crops that led to the rapid growth, and for much of its existence, Durham has been a blue-collar town built around the tobacco industry.

Durham grew quickly; in 1881, the population was just 2,100, but six years later, it more than tripled to 7,128. The growth of the restaurant industry

In 1940, photographer Jack Delano of the Farm Service Administration captured the neon glow of George's Grill at 536 East Main. The building survived until 2008, when it was torn down to make way for a parking lot. *Courtesy of the Library of Congress.*

In the 1940s, Miles restaurant on Roxboro Road served barbecue and other southern staples. The building later became the home of Leo's Seafood #2 and now houses Saigon Grill. *Courtesy of the Durham County Library, North Carolina Collection.*

PROCTOR & CO'.S
RESTAURANT,
117 and 119 PARRISH STREET.

HAPPY AS A LORD ON
THANKSGIVING DAY

Is the man who sees placed before him the National bird in all his juicy and tempting voluptuousness, brown as a berry and done to a turn. We will have some of the finest corn and bread fed turkeys, with flesh as sweet and tender as good food can make it, and fat enough to make them luscious and well flavored. Oysters and all delicacies of the season. Give us your order ahead of time if you can.

W. M. MANSON, Chef.

One of the best in the city and who knows how to get up a dinner right. Go 'round and let him serve you.

An 1899 advertisement for Thanksgiving at Proctor & Co.'s Restaurant that appeared in the *Durham Sun.* Apparently, due to new restrictions passed by the city, Proctor's closed in 1902 after being in business for twelve years. The *Sun* reported, "It is unfortunate for the public that the last white restaurant in the city is to be closed. This was a great accommodation to those who did not care to stop at hotels of boarding houses. This leaves only colored restaurants, outside of the places we have mentioned. The public will be greatly inconvenienced." *Courtesy of Digital NC.*

did not keep up, as the 1887 city guide listed only five restaurants: G.W. Atkinson, B. Green and J.T. Wilkins & Co. (which was also a store) were all located on Mangum Street, while the other two listed eating establishments, T.P. Capps and Alex Craig, were in Hayti on Parrish and Church Streets. Of course, restaurants played a different role in society then, as most people ate at home. In 1887, the number of cooks in the city, most of whom were employed in private homes, was just 119. By comparison, the city had 8 well diggers, 8 tinsmiths, 11 shoemakers and, to keep the heads of women appropriately covered, 12 milliners.

Soon, however, numerous diners, luncheonettes and cafés were established to feed the rapidly increasing number of workers in the cigarette factories and textile mills, as well as tobacco farmers who brought their crops to town to sell in the huge warehouses that once dominated the city. As industry grew, Durham's population rose from less than seven thousand in 1900 to over eighteen thousand in 1910. Owning a restaurant became a much more viable business option with so many more mouths to feed. While tobacco may have been king for over a century, Durham is also home to prestigious Duke University. Over the years, a number of restaurants thrived because they were able to become popular student hangouts. Another important element of Durham's culture has always been the African American community. Because Durham had a burgeoning middle-class black population—thanks to the presence of large black-owned businesses, like North Carolina Mutual Insurance, and a prominent black college—many restaurants sprang up to serve it. The area known as Hayti, in particular, was home to many long-lasting restaurants.

The story of the restaurant industry in Durham is one of racial strife, urban decay and stunning rebirth. As with all southern cities, Durham's restaurants were racially segregated by law until the mid-1960s. Many establishments served both black and white customers but had separate

On Sunday, August 12, 1962, after a Freedom Rally at St. Joseph's AME Church, a reported crowd of five hundred people left the church in a caravan of cars and drove to Howard Johnson's on Durham–Chapel Hill Boulevard. There, they demonstrated in the parking lot against the restaurant's segregation policy. *Photo by Harold Moore. Courtesy of the Durham Herald Collection, University of North Carolina–Chapel Hill.*

Welcome North Carolina College Alumni And Fans

We have planned a very special appetizing Homecoming Menu for you !!!
See our New Dining Room — **THE JADE ROOM** — We are going to give you
the finest in Food in the right atmosphere, Courteous, Quick and Efficient Service

THE SOUTH'S FINEST EATING ESTABLISHMENT
THE DO-NUT SHOP

336 E. PETTIGREW STREET   DIAL 6-0842

W. G. PEARSON, Manager

The Do-Nut Shop was founded in the mid-1940s by George Logan in the Hayti neighborhood. Logan, who also owned the Regal Theater next door, soon named his son-on-law, W.G. "Bill" Pearson, manager of the restaurant. The Do-Nut Shop had the ability to seat over sixty-eight people, and it had a banquet room next door that could hold one hundred people, the green and pink Jade Room. This ad is from the late 1940s. Interestingly, Pearson, who had graduated from what is now North Carolina Central University, eventually decided to go back to law school. He became a practicing lawyer, and the site of the Do-Nut Shop was his office. In the mid-1970s, Pearson became the first black district court judge in Durham. *Courtesy of Andre Vann.*

entrances for both. On February 8, 1960, a group of black students from North Carolina College (now North Carolina Central University) began protesting the segregated lunch counter service at the F.W. Woolworth's department store downtown. They attempted to expand the protest to S.H. Kress and Walgreen's, but Kress was able to close its store before they arrived, and Walgreen's roped off its lunch area. These protests eventually expanded and led to similar efforts elsewhere.

On May 18, 1963, demonstrations were held across Durham. Protesters targeted several restaurants, the courthouse and city hall. Dealing with these protests was the first issue on the agenda of newly elected mayor Wense Grabarek. He appointed a committee to resolve the city's racial tensions, and he made the bold move of appointing Harvey Rape, owner of the popular Harvey's Cafeteria, to the committee. Rape had been vehemently opposed to desegregation, but apparently, Grabarek felt if he could change

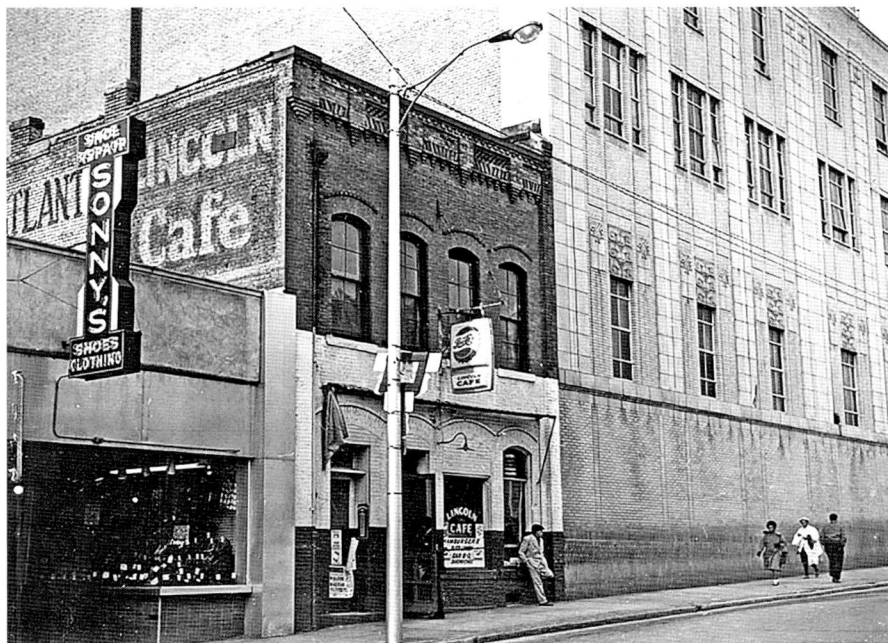

The Lincoln Café at 114 South Mangum Street, directly behind the Kress building, was run by Greek immigrants Mike Galifianakis and Peter Ligets for many years. It primarily served African American clientele. Galifianakis was the father of Congressman Nick Galifianakis and grandfather of comedian Zach Galifianakis, and Ligets was the grandfather of Durham restaurateur Gray Brooks. The Lincoln Café was yet another victim of urban renewal in the late 1960s. *Courtesy of the Durham Herald Collection, University of North Carolina–Chapel Hill.*

Rape's mind, then other dissenters would follow. The plan worked, and Rape agreed to desegregate his dining room. Within a few months, segregation had ended in most of Durham's restaurants.

Interestingly, Durham did have what was probably one of the only integrated lunch counters in the South during the 1950s. Mutt Evans, who served for six terms as the mayor of Durham, owned Evans's United Department Store on Main Street; a judge told Evans he would need to follow the law and segregate his counter. Evans, whose lawyer had researched the issue, replied that the law only applied when customers were seated; the judge agreed, and Evans was able to maintain a desegregated counter by removing the stools and raising the counter to elbow height.

A controversial urban renewal initiative in the late 1960s essentially destroyed much of Durham's historic and cultural fabric and brought about the end of many of the city's longtime restaurants. The construction of the Durham Freeway resulted in the loss of numerous historic buildings and damaged neighborhoods from Hayti to West Durham. Many other buildings in the downtown area were also torn down in the name of progress. Though these changes were supposedly made with good intentions, the result was the demise of the once-bustling city center. A few restaurants took a chance on downtown in the 1970s, such as Sudi's at 11 West Main, but as the customer base in the area declined, success was hard to find. Even longtime downtown restaurants like the Palms gave up their downtown locations in the early 1980s. While the city did experience growth in its southern quarter and toward its neighbor Chapel Hill to the west, it wasn't until the late 1990s that Durham's downtown area truly began to reawaken.

Beginning in the 1940s, the Nance family operated many restaurants around Durham. Among them were Mayola's Grill, which was operated by Mayola Nance (later Smith), and Top Hat Grill on Broad Street, which was owned by her son Maitland. These 1970s ads from the *Duke Chronicle* are for two other Maitland Nance–owned restaurants: Nance Cafeteria, which was located where Durham Bulls Athletic Park is today; and Nance Seafood, which was located in the building that was once Turnage's Barbecue on Morrene Road. *Collection of the author.*

MAYOLA'S CHILI HOUSE

BREAKFAST — LUNCH — DINNER
OPEN 6 A. M. CLOSE 12 P. M.

WELCOME
TO THE
GOLDEN ROOM

"A HOME AWAY FROM HOME"

109 N. GREGSON ST.   PHONE 9-2256

Left: Mayola's Chili House was a popular burger and beer destination for Duke students in the 1960s. This ad is from *Hill's 1961 Durham City Guide. Courtesy of Digital NC.*

Below: From the late 1940s to the mid-1950s, 111 South Dillard Street was home to Barfield's Restaurant. Run by Pauline Barfield (*far left*), the establishment was located across the street from Sears. By the late 1950s, the building housed Bill's Café before it became a seafood market in the 1960s. *Courtesy of Dawn Robson.*

CLIP THIS COUPON
DINNER SPECIAL
50¢ off
Coupon Good through May 12, 1985

with coupon (spicy or regular recipe)
*one coupon per dinner

Good on any combo
2 pcs. Dinner
3 pcs. Dinner
4 pcs. Dinner
Chicken Fried Steak

Free Deliveries
Minimum order $75

PeteRinaldis
FRIED CHICKEN

Taking Care of Chicken Business

Landsakes "IT'S GOOD"

2801 GUESS RD.— ¼ MILE NORTH OF I-85
Hours: Mon-Sat 6 a.m.-10 p.m.
Sun 8 a.m.-10 p.m.

CLIP THIS COUPON

In the 1940s and 1950s, Pete and Arline Rinaldi ran Rinaldi's Grill. Located on the southeast corner of Peabody and West Main Streets, the restaurant was popular with Duke students for its burgers. It closed in the late 1950s, but in 1963, Pete Jr. opened the city's first Kentucky Fried Chicken franchise on Ninth Street. He eventually owned several franchises before he sold them in 1969. In 1979, he launched Pete Rinaldi's Fried Chicken on Guess Road, with his friend Colonel Harlan Sanders reportedly in attendance for the grand opening. *Courtesy of the Durham Herald Collection, University of North Carolina–Chapel Hill.*

For much of Durham's restaurant history, its dining establishments have offered similar menus. Most have been based on traditional southern cooking (pork barbecue, Brunswick stew, et cetera), fried seafood and burgers and hotdogs. For special nights out, diners would visit one of the city's steakhouses. A 1913 article on the opening of the Star Café on Parrish Street in the *Durham Sun* even made a point of stating that, at the establishment, "everything will be cooked in the southern style." Slowly, however, the flavors of other, non-Southern places, such as China and Italy, became options. True fine dining began appearing in Durham in the 1980s. Innovative restaurants such as Anotherthyme and Magnolia Grill—true, chef-driven establishments—paved the way for the city's culinary renaissance. Though there were definitely bright spots in the Durham culinary scene through the 1990s, they were few and far between.

By the early 2000s, downtown Durham was beginning to experience another period of revitalization. Businesses returned to long-empty storefronts, and many of the red brick tobacco buildings were renovated. Gary Kueber, creator of the Open Durham history website, recalled those early years of downtown's rebirth.

> *Opening a restaurant is always a risky endeavor, but when someone did that downtown early on, people would react with a "bless their hearts." You had to cross the dark hulks of the tobacco factories to get to it, and I think that was a bridge too far for a lot of people.*

In 1974, two vintage railroad cars were trucked to Durham to create a steakhouse at Lakewood Shopping Center. By 1977, the cars were for sale again, and the new owner moved them to Guess Road, just off Interstate 85 and behind the Carolina-Duke Motor Inn. There, a new restaurant called the Wabash Express—named after the train the cars came from—opened. It remained in business for over a decade. *Photo by Jim Sparks. Courtesy of the Durham Herald Collection, University of North Carolina–Chapel Hill.*

Joe and Jo's was one of the first ones east of Brightleaf. That was an interesting point in time, about 2004 and 2005. Joe and Jo's really had some staying power until the Joe and the Jo got divorced. The restaurant closed and was supplanted by Bull McCabe's. But it was a really interesting gathering spot. I think from that group, I can see a line where people told a friend that Durham was cool, and they told a friend, and word spread. I very distinctly remember this experience from a couple years later, probably 2009, sitting outside at Bull McCabe's. I had this sudden realization that there were people walking on the sidewalks downtown. It just struck me because I was like, "I don't think I've ever seen this before." People walking, not hurriedly going from the bank to their cars, but they were just ambling. It's funny to think about now, but a few years before that, there just were no people downtown.

Restaurants definitely led the way in Durham's return to downtown. Rue Cler and Piedmont opened downtown in 2006 in areas that had long been devoid of dining options. Both were highly acclaimed, and *Condé*

Nast Traveler even included Piedmont on its Hot List of the world's best new restaurants. It called the eatery's cuisine "an appealing combination of farm-fresh earnestness and contemporary style." Following the lead of these two restaurants, others soon followed; among them was Revolution, which moved into the former Baldwin department store building, one of the first large structures to be renovated. People returned to the city center, and downtown became the place to be. More restaurants, that offered a wide range of cuisines, were launched to support the growth of the city. Despite these changes, Durham remained true to its roots. Today, diners can still find traditional pork barbecue and a Carolina-style hotdog, but they can also enjoy flavors from around the world and unique farm-to-fork creations from award-winning chefs.

In 2008, *Bon Appétit* magazine named Durham, along with its neighbor Chapel Hill, "America's Foodiest Small Town." The recognition continued,

Chef Mark Day worked at Fowler's Gourmet in Brightleaf Square before leaving to open his own acclaimed bistro, Mark's at Five Points, in 1987. In 1993, the bistro became Mark's New American Cuisine. In the mid-1990s, Day left the restaurant world to focus on catering; his former building later became home to Joe & Jo's and is currently home to Bull McCabe's. *Courtesy of the Durham Herald Collection, University of North Carolina–Chapel Hill.*

and the resurgence of the city's restaurant industry earned even greater acclaim in 2013, when *Southern Living* magazine declared Durham the "Tastiest Town in the South." In the rankings, Durham prevailed over larger cities such as New Orleans, Atlanta and Memphis. In the same year, the city had four semi-finalists in the annual James Beard Foundation awards—the top honors in the food world. There is no denying that Durham arrived as a nationally acclaimed restaurant town.

Chef Ricky Moore, a native of Eastern North Carolina, graduated from the Culinary Institute of America in New York. His culinary career then took him to France, Chicago and Washington D.C., and he even appeared on the Food Network's *Iron Chef America* in 2007. When Moore decided to open his own restaurant in 2012, he chose Durham as its location. Moore said, "I saw something in Durham I had seen before up north, a city changing and growing with new infrastructure and lots of opportunity. But all of the history in the city was really important to me as well," he continued. "There has always been a great entrepreneurial spirit in Durham and, with regard to restaurants, a lot of chef ownership. People in the city are very supportive of homegrown businesses, and a lot of good things were happening." Moore's first Saltbox Seafood Joint opened on Mangum Street, and he opened his second restaurant in the former Shrimp Boats location in 2017.

Along with the positive changes in the city, there was some loss. With more restaurants, competition grew, and inevitably, some could not compete. "The thing about competition is that it isn't just limited to your set," said Don Ball, former owner of Papagayo. "There are always hot restaurants that pull people away, but even a mid-scale restaurant—if they are packing the house—is taking away people who might come eat with you. It's a math equation in many ways, because there is just so much population and so many seats in town." And the restaurant business is tough—some owners just decide to change careers or even retire. When a favorite restaurant closes for whatever reason, it leaves a void in the community, and only the memories of it remain. "For those of us who have lived in Durham for more than a decade, it feels like a different town," said Chris Reid, a food writer and former restaurant reviewer for the blog *Carpe Durham*. "We try to keep the torch alive for the Bull City of even a few years ago—venturing into the grand old house that was Four Square, seeking out a spot at the long, lively bar at Magnolia, singing sea shanties in the upstairs bar of Fishmongers," she continued. "We wax poetic about yesterday's Durham while dining in the likes of Mateo, the Durham and Pizzeria Toro." As time passes and change continues, it also becomes difficult to remember everything that was in Durham. One of the goals of this book is to document the locations of some of Durham's much-missed eating establishments.

Will Durham remain a culinary trendsetter? It is impossible to know, but the city remains an innovative leader in terms of its restaurants. Creative menus and new flavors are just a few ways to move restaurants forward, but there are others, including the food truck trend of the past decade or so. While they may not be restaurants in the truest sense of the word, food trucks have become an integral part of Durham's dining culture. Customers have their favorites and travel to their temporary locations to find them. In fact, food trucks have been important in forming many new "brick and mortar" restaurants. OnlyBurger began as a food truck in 2008; only after it proved to be popular as a food truck was there a true OnlyBurger restaurant opened on Shannon Road in 2010. This was followed by another location outside the Durham Bulls Athletic Park. The pizzas from Pie Pushers' truck were also very popular; after five years of operating as a truck, Pie Pushers expanded with a permanent location on West Main Street in 2016.

Whatever the future may hold for Durham, keep in mind that the bar for restaurants in the city was set pretty high one hundred years ago. In 1920, the Phoenix Café, which was located across from the courthouse at 205 East Main, had the slogan "Honestly, it is the *best* place to eat." Ads also proclaimed that the establishment was "Sanitary—Up-to-Date in Every Respect." It is certainly a challenge for restaurants to live up to their predecessors when they are competing with such a grandiose proclamation as that.

1.
Feeding the Farmers

If Durham is known for one thing above all others, it is tobacco. Because of the crop, Durham went from a rural train stop to a booming industrial town in just a few decades. By the early 1900s, tobacco and tobacco products had made Durham world-famous. To support the tobacco business, a unique part of Durham's food service industry evolved.

During every fall, beginning in 1871, farmers brought their crops to town to sell at auction, which took place in one of the huge warehouses that were once located just north of downtown. As they waited for their crops to reach the auctioneer—sometimes, they had to wait for a couple of days—the farmers had to eat. To feed them, the warehouses set up cafés; there, farmers, tobacco buyers and everyone associated with the market ate their meals (and drank their beer). Outside of the warehouses, a few other restaurants—as well as a few pool halls and street vendors—catered primarily to those who came to town for the purpose of selling or buying tobacco.

As a part of Roosevelt's New Deal, the U.S. Farm Security Administration was created. Included in its mission was a stated effort to document the lives of farmers and the challenges they faced during the Depression. To do this kind of documentation, the FSA hired young photographers—many of whom became some of the country's most famous photojournalists—and dispatched them across the United States. Between 1936 and 1940, the agency sent photographers Arthur Rothstein, Marion Post Wolcott and Jack Delano to Durham to document the tobacco auctions and farm life in the surrounding area. Among the

The warehouse district just north of downtown. The Palms restaurant can be seen in the foreground. *Photo by Arthur Rothstein. Courtesy of the Library of Congress.*

Farmers Café, with its segregated entrances, was located on Rigsbee Street. As it was very close to the warehouse district, it was geared toward serving those who came to town to sell their crops. *Photo by Jack Delano. Courtesy of the Library of Congress.*

The Mangum Café. *Photo by Jack Delano. Courtesy of the Library of Congress.*

Liberty Café. *Photo by Marion Post Wolcott. Courtesy of the Library of Congress.*

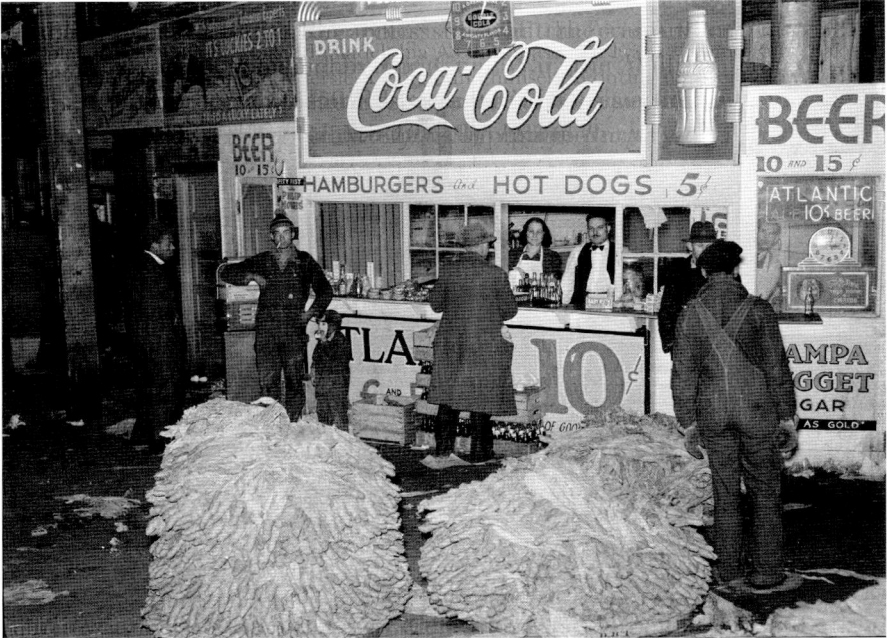

Café inside the Roycroft warehouse at 401 Rigsbee Avenue in 1939. *Photo by Marion Post Wolcott. Courtesy of the Library of Congress.*

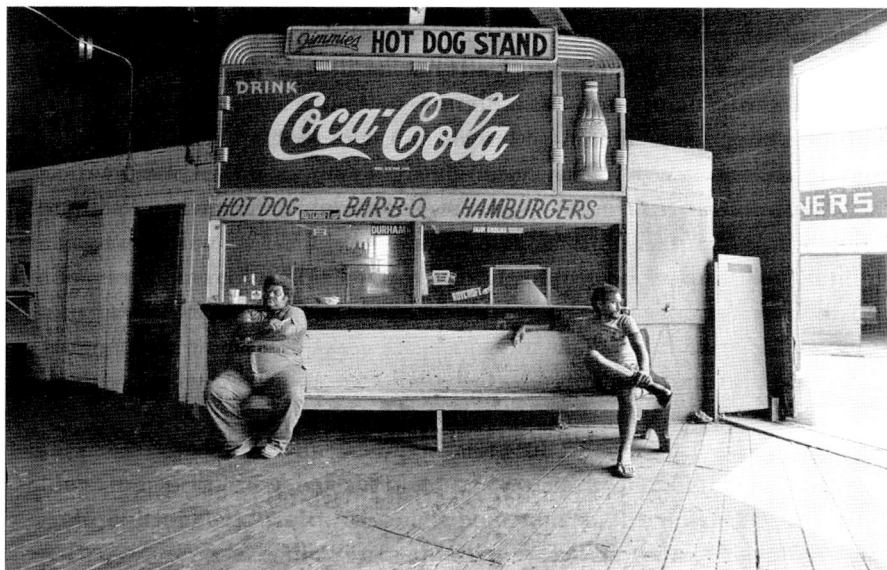

The tobacco markets were beginning to die out by the 1980s and with them went market cafés. Customers were obviously lacking in this 1982 image of the hot dog stand inside the Roycroft warehouse. *Courtesy of the Jerome Friar Photographic Collection, University of North Carolina–Chapel Hill.*

many photos they took, there are several of cafés and their patrons inside the warehouse buildings.

The last tobacco auctions were held in the mid-1980s. Not long after, in 1987, American Tobacco closed its Durham operations and left behind a score of empty buildings and unemployed workers. When Liggett and Myers moved the last of their operations out of Durham in 1999, the city was essentially left with no presence in the tobacco industry for the first time in over 130 years. One by one, the huge warehouses that had once dominated the city were torn down for new development. With them, a very important part of Durham disappeared.

2.
The Underappreciated Hotdog

While barbecue, steak and fried chicken have always been constants in Durham's restaurant history, the one food that may have had the biggest impact is the humble hotdog. Like North Carolina barbecue (yes, both styles—Eastern and Lexington), one of the state's cultural food treasures is the Carolina hotdog. Across the country, one can find hotdogs with a wide range of toppings and condiments, but for a Carolina dog, the rules are pretty simple. The base is a bright red hotdog, usually the Bright Leaf brand that has been made in Smithfield, North Carolina, since 1941. The toppings are limited to chili, mustard, onions and slaw. Some establishments offer their own special additions, like cheese, but loyalists say that this is straying into foreign territory.

Many North Carolina towns have their own famous hotdog establishments (such as Bill's in Washington, Zack's in Burlington and Dick's in Wilson), and residents will argue over which is best. Durham is no different; and over the years, its hotdog grills and cafés have been considered among the best in the state. Some famous Durham lunch places, such as Wimpy's and King's, include tasty hotdogs in their offerings, but others have become almost solely dedicated to the art of the wiener-filled bun. There is no way to know when the first hotdogs were offered in Durham, but the small restaurant section of the 1920 city guide lists Toney's Wienie Shop at 331 West Main Street, Mike's Wienie Stand at 341 West Main Street, Five Point Wienie Stand at 102 Morris Street and Steve's Wienie Stand at 311 West Main Street.

The original Amos 'N' Andy's, shown here in 1957, was on the bottom floor of the Strudwick building on Chapel Hill Street. *Courtesy of the Durham Herald Collection, University of North Carolina–Chapel Hill.*

Information about these restaurants is scarce, but one can surmise that they were establishments that specialized in hotdogs. (Mike's Wienie Stand was owned by Mike Galifianakis, who would later run the Lincoln Café for years.)

One place that still holds a special place in the hearts (and stomachs) of older Durham residents is Amos 'n' Andy. Opened in the early 1930s by P.P. Pool, the original Amos 'n' Andy was located in the 200 block of East Chapel Hill Street, where the Marriot stands today. Norris Eubanks began working there in 1943 at age seventeen, and he eventually became half-owner. He became sole owner in 1957, when Pool died and left him his half of the business. "At Amos 'n' Andy's the hotdogs were great and the chili was great," said Mike Knowles, who grew up in Durham in the 1950s. "They were famous for how quick they could slap them together, 'Here's your two—here's your two.' They were doing two things at once. You got them and paid at the countertop, but you could sit in there and eat, too. And it was cheap." If the stools were full at Amos 'n' Andy's, patrons sat on Pepsi crates to enjoy their dogs topped with homemade chili and slaw. On the wall was a photo of two Duke football players who tied—at seventeen—in a hotdog eating contest in 1959. Interestingly, Amos 'n' Andy even served beer, which was uncommon for hotdog-centric lunch establishments. When Norris Eubanks passed away in 1973, his son Johnny took over. Later in the 1970s, the business moved near the intersection of Highways 54 and 55. A couple of years after Johnny's untimely death in 1981, the family sold the business. Despite being gone for over thirty years, Amos 'n' Andy's chili is still praised. In 2003, the *Durham Herald-Sun* published what is purported to be the correct recipe.

Amos 'n' Andy Chili

INGREDIENTS:
2 pounds of hamburger, divided
1 quart of water
1 medium onion, grated
5 cloves of garlic, crushed
2 tablespoons of chili powder (adjust to taste)
1 tablespoon of cumin
1 tablespoon of paprika
2 teaspoons of salt
1 teaspoon of ground cayenne pepper (optional—adjust to taste)

Place a pound of the hamburger in a saucepan with the water, and squish it to form a slurry. Crumble the other pound of hamburger in a frying pan and brown well. Remove the meat to the saucepan and sauté the onion and garlic in the remaining grease for about five minutes. Place onion, garlic, grease and all the spices in the saucepan with the slurry. Bring to a boil, then turn back and simmer for 2½ hours, until consistency is right for spreading on a hotdog. You can also prepare this in a Crock Pot, instead of a saucepan, using four hours on high, or eight hours on low.

In east Durham, Paschall's Grill (also called Paschall's Café) was the place to go for hotdogs. Located at 1102 Holloway Street in a 1920s building that had previously housed a small grocery and at least a couple of different grills (Lane's and Carter's), Paschall's began serving hotdogs in 1964.

Right: Herman Paschall at work at his grill in 1979. *Photo by Tony Rumple. Courtesy of the Durham Herald Collection, University of North Carolina–Chapel Hill.*

Below: The Hillsborough Road location of the Dog House. *Photo by Chris Holaday.*

Owner Herman Paschall was a former textile worker who gained his first restaurant experience working in a tobacco warehouse café. He went on to work at R&M Café and Edgemont Lunch, and eventually, he ran the concession stand in Durham Hosiery Mill #6 before opening his own establishment. At his grill, Paschall made a still-remembered chili for his 'dogs that attracted a largely blue-collar lunch crowd from the surrounding area. Herman Paschall died in 1981, but his family—most notably, his daughter-in-law Hilda—continued to run the grill. With a faded sign and a location in a part of town that had languished, many passersby would have thought Pascall's was closed, but the restaurant remained acclaimed among connoisseurs of the Carolina dog. It quietly closed for good in 2012.

Several other establishments in Durham were also known for their hotdogs. Edgemont Lunch at 911 East Main Street served hotdogs to a generation of textile workers at the Durham Hosiery mills and the Golden Belt Hosiery Mill in the 1940s and 1950s. Joyland Grill, which was located at the corner of Holloway and Junction Roads, was run by Norman and Ruby Pope. After becoming famous for its hotdogs and plate lunches and after serving for over thirty years, Joyland Grill fell victim to road expansion in 2005. Hazel's Hotdogs closed in 1997, but it made lasting memories. "My grandparents lived off Avondale, and I remember, as a kid in the late seventies and early eighties, walking over to Hazel's from their house to get hotdogs,' said Lance Sawyers. "She was this elderly lady who made really good hotdogs at amazing prices. My mother would even go there sometimes and come back with an armful to feed us kids."

The current king of the Durham hotdog scene is the Dog House. Founded in 1971 by Stuart Henderson, with one distinctive dog house–shaped building on Miami Boulevard, the chain grew to ten locations. Today, there are still four locations in Durham. The other hotdog specialist in Durham is Jimmy's Famous Hotdogs. Owned by the founder of Spartacus, Jimmy's entered the market in 2011. Today, it has two Durham locations.

3.
New Flavors

For much of its culinary history, Durham has been a city built by meat-and-three diners, steakhouses and barbecue joints. Even in the age of segregation, the food offerings were pretty much the same, regardless of whether the patrons were black or white. Meals based on good Southern-style cooking were really all the offerings available. The Oriental was likely the first restaurant to serve any type of meal in Durham that fell outside the "Southern" category when it opened in 1938. Twenty years later, Annamaria's brought pizza, spaghetti and other common Italian dishes to the city, even if they were somewhat Americanized. Annamaria's was soon followed by the Pizza Palace.

With the popularity of the Oriental, Chinese cuisine slowly began to spread through the city. For several years, in the early to mid-1950s, city guides listed Asia Café at 611 Fayetteville Street in Hayti as another dining option. During the 1960s and 1970s, however, a number of restaurants began to offer Chinese cuisine. K.C. Hung's China Inn at 2701 Hillsborough Road opened in 1975; it went through several owners and reincarnations before closing in the early 2000s. Shanghai Restaurant opened in the 1980s at 3433 Hillsborough Road and is still thriving. Hong Kong restaurant on Guess Road opened in the late 1980s and is still the place to go for dim sum. On the weekends, Hong Kong's staff comes by with carts filled with small plates of unusual offerings. In 1990, Diana and Oliver Yu opened Neo-China at 4015 University Drive, which specializes in Sichuan cuisine. The restaurant's upscale presentation of Chinese food was popular, and the

Right: In the late 1960s, 408 Morgan Street housed Moon Restaurant. By 1972, it had become Four Seas; it then became the Peking Restaurant before it was torn down to make way for a parking lot in 1986. *Courtesy of the Durham Herald Collection, University of North Carolina–Chapel Hill.*

Below: Hong Kong Restaurant in 1990. *Photo by Harold Moore. Courtesy of the Durham Herald Collection, University of North Carolina–Chapel Hill.*

couple expanded to other locations in Cary and North Raleigh. In 2019, *Indy Week* named Happy China on Durham–Chapel Hill Boulevard the Best Chinese Restaurant in Durham County; Shanghai and Neo-China were finalists for the honor.

As diners became familiar and comfortable with Chinese food, it paved the way for flavors from the other parts of Asia. One of the first Japanese restaurants in Durham was Yamazushi. It was followed by others, including Kanki on Mt. Moriah Road, which opened in 2002. Bahn's opened in 1988 and offered Chinese as well as Vietnamese dishes, and Saigon Grill on North Roxboro Road became known for its traditional Vietnamese *pho*. Thai food was hard to find in the area until a brother-and-sister team from Thailand, Oddy Tacha and Kanchana Techarukphong, opened Thai Café on University Drive in 2007. Even Mongolian food came to Durham in 2003, when the Bali-Hai Mongolian Grill opened on Ninth Street. Today, Asian food in Durham has even gone upscale with restaurants such as M Sushi and Dashi, a Japanese ramen shop with an *izakaya*, a traditional Japanese pub, upstairs.

The popularity of European fare in Durham didn't stop with the large number of Italian restaurants that opened in the city. The unique cuisines of other countries also gained representation. Parizäde started offering a wide variety of Mediterranean dishes in 1990, and Spartacus began serving Greek specialties soon afterward. Mateo Bar de Tapas is currently one of the city's most highly acclaimed restaurants, and it features the small dishes that are so popular in Spain. Led by chef Matt Kelly, Mateo Bar de Tapas was a semifinalist in the running for the 2013 James Beard Award for the best new restaurant in the country.

Other restaurants with a European flare in Durham include Guglhupf, which opened in the late 1990s as a German bakery. In 2004, Guglhupf expanded into a full-scale restaurant, where owner Claudia Kemmet-Cooper, who was formally trained as a baker in Munich, could show off the traditional dishes of her home country. The James Joyce, an Irish pub, opened across the street from Brightleaf Square in 1998 and served traditional Irish pub fare. "The James Joyce was vibrant in the early 2000s—filled with Irish accents—the food, drink and camaraderie felt genuine," said Josh Wittman, who eventually opened the Federal next door. "It was dark and brooding and made you feel transported to a small town in Ireland. As many a day (and night) was spent there, it would be right to give the Joyce a lot of credit for helping to inspire what was soon to be the Federal."

Claudia Kemmet-Cooper and partner, Hartmut Jahn, in the kitchen of Guglhupf in 1998. *Photo by Ellen Ozier. Courtesy of the Durham Herald Collection, University of North Carolina–Chapel Hill.*

The first culinary representative from Africa in Durham was the Palace International, which opened in 1989. When Friesh Dabei opened Blue Nile on Chapel Hill Road in 1994, it was the first Ethiopian restaurant in the state. It closed after a decade (Dabei focused on her Queen of Sheba restaurant in Chapel Hill), but in 2017, cousins Fasil Tesfaye and Zewditu Zewdie brought Ethiopian cuisine back to the city when they opened Goorsha on West Main Street.

The first Indian cuisine served in Durham may have come from the Sallam Cultural Center in the late 1970s. Run by musician Brother Yusuf Salim and three partners, the center was part–jazz club and part-restaurant, serving vegetarian platters. The West Chapel Hill Street building later became the Durham Food Co-op, which was transformed into the Cookery, a kitchen available for rent, in 2001. (The Cookery became an incubator that helped start several local food trucks and restaurants.) Other restaurants that helped bring Indian fare to Durham in the 1990s were Suman's and Dale's. In 1998, Sitar India Palace began serving southern Indian cuisine in what was known as Regency Plaza, and it soon became a fixture in the Durham culinary scene. When the strip mall met its demise in 2009, Sitar moved to the former site of the Lone Star Steakhouse at 3630 Durham Chapel Hill Boulevard. There, it has remained popular, and its patrons can even enjoy music from its namesake instrument on the weekends. An offshoot of Sitar even operates at Duke University's Broadhead Center, where it serves hundreds of students each day.

Surprisingly, the 1990 guide that was put out by the Durham Convention and Visitors Bureau listed only four Mexican restaurants: Tijuana Fats, Papagayo, Jacaranda's and El Rodeo. That number has grown immensely, as the demographics of the city have also changed throughout the 1990s and the 2000s. New arrivals brought many new flavors with them, which Durhamites soon discovered they enjoyed as well. Like Chinese food, the first Mexican dishes available in the city were commonly known—such as enchiladas and refried beans—and appealed to a largely American clientele. That soon changed, and now, the Mexican food category in Durham includes numerous Mexican restaurants and taquerias. These establishments include Roselia Flores's Super Taqueria on North Roxboro Street, which opened in 2001; there, one can find obscure specialties and diverse offerings, including *lengua* tacos with *horchata* to drink.

The influx of restaurants that got their inspiration from south of the border didn't stop at Mexican cuisine. La Cacerola on Guess Road specializes in Honduran cuisine, El Chapin on Durham–Chapel Hill Boulevard features Guatemalan dishes and El Cuscatleco on Garrett Road offers *pupusas* from El Savador. From farther south still, Mi Peru on University Drive offers roasted chicken and *lomo saltado* from its namesake country; and Chamas Churrascaria, a Brazilian steakhouse in Brightleaf Square, opened in 2004 and operated for over decade before closing. Gary Kueber recalled:

> I remember a small South American restaurant called El Inca on Main Street, I think where Taberna Tapas is now. I would not remember that so distinctly, but in 2001, we had a huge snow storm. The power was out almost everywhere except in the core of the downtown loop, where the power lines were buried. The experience of downtown at that time was that there were not many people at all and it was empty, but I remember me and my ex-girlfriend trudging through the snow to El Inca. The place was packed to the gills because they had power and heat. We were all huddled in there, drinking warm coffee. I don't remember there being other places to choose from in downtown then; it may have been the only one.

Diners could also take a trip to the islands by visiting Jamaica Jamaica on Highway 55 for Caribbean dishes, or they could visit one of the Cuban restaurants that had popped up. Cuban Revolution opened in the American Tobacco complex in 2009 as the second location of a restaurant franchise from Providence, Rhode Island; it closed in 2019. The Old Havana Sandwich Shop featured the famed sandwiches of the island for several years before the owners decided to move a block west on Main Street and transformed into COPA, which is also Cuban-themed. A restaurant that has combined all of these culinary styles for over twenty years is the Blue Corn Café on Ninth Street, which has the self-stated mission of serving "fusion style flavor" from the Caribbean and all of Latin and South America.

New flavors did not only travel from foreign lands to Durham. The 1990s saw the arrival of dishes from Louisiana in Durham, first with the opening of Crescent Café in 1990. It was run by the chefs and owners Walter Royal and Don Wexell (Royal was a Magnolia Grill alumnus who won the Food Network's *Iron Chef America* competition in 2006). Though highly acclaimed, Crescent Café may have been ahead of its time in regard to the revitalization downtown. Even a *Baltimore Sun* review noted that it was "nestled among several vacant storefronts." It closed after a few years, and the site later became the original home of Dame's Chicken and Waffles. Next was New Orleans Cookery, which opened in 1996. This was the second location of a Chapel Hill restaurant, and it operated in the building that now houses Bull McCabe's. Papa Mojo's Roadhouse, which was run by chef and musician Mel Melton and opened in 2007, served Cajun cuisine and brought nationally known musical acts to its location on Highway 55 for seven years.

Even in the realm of barbecue, challengers from other regions have appeared in Durham to contest North Carolina's sacred pork. Texas native Dan Ferguson, along with his partner, Scott Howell, opened the Original Q Shack in 2003. The restaurant serves pork, but Texas-style beef brisket has kept it popular with Durham's aficionados of smoked meats for over fifteen years.

Not only has Durham witnessed the arrival of foods from elsewhere, but it has also become accustomed to seeing new takes on traditional Southern dishes. Inventive chefs have reinterpreted classics using new ingredients, and they often focus on the ingredients just as much as they do on the final dish. The idea of farm-to-fork and the use of locally gown ingredients are common in many chef-driven restaurants. The diversity offered by Durham restaurants continues to grow and reflect changes in both the city and in the culinary curiosity of its diners.

4.

The Chain

Can a dining establishment that is part of a non-local chain really play an important role in a city's restaurant culture? The easy answer is no, because they are not unique. They bring the exact same food, and often the same building, to cities across the country. On closer examination, however, it is apparent that chain restaurants can be an integral part of any dining scene.

In Durham, several chain restaurants—both regional and national—have had remarkably long lives. Honey's and Shrimp Boats were once parts of regional chains but long survived as independent restaurants even though their chains dissolved. Another regional chain with a Durham location was Do-Nut Dinette, which was located at 1010 West Main Street. Do-Nut Dinette began with several locations in Charlotte in the 1940s and expanded to other North Carolina cities, including Greensboro and Burlington, and it eventually had locations in South Carolina and Virginia. What was probably the last Do-Nut Dinette closed in 2014 in in Norfolk, Virginia. T.K. Tripps—later just Tripps—was part of a Greensboro-based chain that opened its first locations in the early 1980s. Its first Durham location was on Durham–Chapel Hill Boulevard (1990–98), and it opened a second location on West Club Boulevard in 2000. In 2018, that restaurant was transformed into Kickback Jack's, the parent company's other restaurant concept.

Darryl's was also a regional chain that had a presence in Durham. Based in Raleigh, Darryl's 1890 opened on Durham–Chapel Hill Boulevard in 1978, and Darryl's 1881 opened on North Roxboro Street less than two

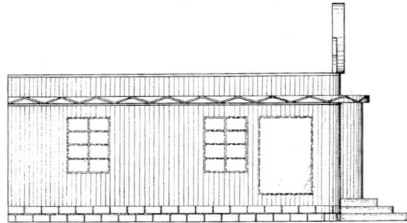

Jan. 2, 1951   A. M. BERRYHILL   Des. 161,413

DINER OR SIMILAR ARTICE

Filed Dec. 27, 1948   2 Sheets-Sheet 1

Fig. 1

Fig. 3

INVENTOR
ALLEN M. BERRYHILL

BY   *Parrott & Richards*

ATTORNEYS

Right: Do-Nut Dinette, a chain based in Charlotte, had a Durham location on Main Street, just west of the Ivy Room. Its design, complete with a shiny metal façade and neon donut sign, was patented in 1951 and used at locations in several states. *Courtesy of the United States Patent Office.*

Below: Customers wait in line for the grand opening of Darryl's 1890 on November 8, 1978. *Photo by Jim Sparks. Courtesy of the Durham Herald Collection, University of North Carolina–Chapel Hill.*

years later. Darryl's was founded in 1971 by Thad Eure Jr. and Charles Winston, the men who established the popular Angus Barn restaurant on Highway 70 between Durham and Raleigh, and Darryl Davis, who owned a Pizza Inn franchise in Raleigh. The first Darryl's opened in Raleigh, and the concept, which included antique décor, soon expanded to other cities across the South. The chain was eventually sold and re-sold, and in the early 2000s, the owner filed for bankruptcy, and Darryl's 1890 was closed by 2002. Darryl's 1890's building was torn down, and Darryl's 1881's site, which was closed in the late 1980s, was the home of GreenField's for a few years before it became Ole NC Barbecue. The site is now a Starbucks Coffee franchise.

How many Durham residents can say that they have never dined at Piccadilly Cafeteria in South Square Mall? Piccadilly, a chain that had its beginnings in Baton Rouge, Louisiana, in 1944, was a fixture at the mall for twenty-seven years. Perhaps it—like most cafeterias—was seen as being a destination for older diners, but from the opening of South Square Mall in 1975 until its closure in 2002, Piccadilly remained popular. On Sunday afternoons, in particular, it was often filled with grandparents, children and grandchildren.

One of the more interesting chains that made an appearance in Durham was Schrafft's. The company began as a candy store in Boston in the 1800s before expanding into restaurants. Schrafft's was particularly popular in New York, where it had several locations. It was known for having a largely female clientele, so in an effort to expand its customer base, the chain opened a few Schrafft's Country Inns. The Durham location, which opened in 1960, was a large colonial-style brick building on Durham–Chapel Hill Boulevard. The experiment did not succeed, however, and by 1966, the restaurant had become Blair House. The site is now occupied by Michael Jordan Nissan.

Among the more nationally recognized chains that have had long presences in Durham, Red Lobster is the oldest. The chain's location on Durham–Chapel Hill Boulevard opened in the spring of 1978. Not far to the west, a Chili's location opened in 1986, while farther down the road, Outback Steakhouse opened a location at New Hope Commons in 1993. At Northgate Mall, Ruby Tuesday's opened a location in 1990. Other large chains that have come and gone in Durham include Joe's Crab Shack (1998–2004), Romano's Macaroni Grill (1994–2009), Grady's American Grill (1996–2004) and On the Border (1999–2008). In the 1970s, California-based Sambo's had two locations in Durham at 3630 Chapel Hill Boulevard and 3500 North Duke Street. The Chapel Hill Boulevard location was eventually taken over by Lone Star Steakhouse (1995–2006), a chain from Winston-

Salem that spread nationwide but is now defunct. The building is now home to Sitar India Palace. These chains and many others have disappeared from Durham for various reasons—sometimes they've had financial problems at the national level, and other times, they just underperformed locally—but all have a place in the restaurant history of Durham.

With regard to chains, we would be remiss if we didn't mention fast-food. The seemingly ubiquitous burger and chicken restaurants, with which we are all so familiar, didn't even exist in Durham until the early 1960s. The first McDonald's in North Carolina opened in Greensboro in 1959, and the chain expanded rapidly. Within a couple of years, it arrived in Durham and opened its first location at the corner of Avondale and North Roxboro Streets. The fast-food craze spread, and other chains—both national and regional, big and small—soon followed. Among them was North Carolina–based Hardeee's. Durham's first Hardee's opened in 1964 at 1212 South Duke Street. Not long after that, Durham's first Kentucky Fried Chicken was opened by Pete Rinaldi at 806 Ninth Street. National fast-food chains, including Florida-based Burger King, soon followed. Later, other North Carolina–based fast-food chains came to Durham, including Bojangles, Biscuitville and Cook Out. The Church's Chicken franchise arrived at 942 North Miami Boulevard in 1978. It may be Durham's longest extant fast-food restaurant that is still in its original location. Love them or not, fast-food franchises have become an important dining element in every city.

5

Dining at the Hotel

Hotels are primarily thought of as places for lodging, but many also include dining options for guests and the public. Dining at hotels was a continuation of the tradition of serving meals at boardinghouses, but as the city grew, true hotels with full-service restaurants began to appear. One of the earliest Durham hotels to serve meals to the public was the Malbourne, which was located at 223 East Main Street and built in 1912. In its early years, the Malbourne was the place to go for Sunday dinner, which, in 1915, cost sixty cents—unless a diner preferred the "sizzling steak with French-fried potatoes and tomatoes," which raised the price to seventy-five cents. As late as 1960, when the Malbourne was well past its prime, it was still advertising its Coffee Shoppe, which offered "Club Breakfast–Lunches and Dinners. Also, A La Carte Service." In 1966, the Malbourne was yet another victim of urban renewal, and it was torn down along with the entire block.

At the corner of East Chapel Hill and Corcoran Streets, the sixteen-story, three-hundred-room Washington Duke Hotel was constructed in 1924 and 1925. At the time of its construction, not only was the Washington Duke Hotel the tallest building in the city, but it also offered Durham a new level of luxury in lodging and dining. Over the course of fifty years, the hotel was the site of countless business lunches and dinners, banquets and other formal dining occasions. For much of that time, the hotel could arguably have been considered the most important dining spot in the city. With

WASHINGTON DUKE HOTEL, DURHAM, N. C.   107454

A 1920s postcard showing the new Washington Duke Hotel. *Courtesy of the Durwood Barbour Postcard Collection, University of North Carolina–Chapel Hill.*

The Malbourne Hotel in the 1950s. The coffee shop restaurant was entered on the North Roxboro Street side of the building. *Photo by Charles Cooper. Courtesy of the Durham Herald Collection, University of North Carolina–Chapel Hill.*

business dwindling and its building in need of repairs, the Washington Duke was demolished in 1975 (a very unfortunate decision with regard to the historical fabric of the city), and downtown Durham was left without a luxury hotel.

The twenty-room Biltmore Hotel at 330 East Pettigrew Street in Hayti was built around 1929. In its heyday, the Biltmore was one of the most renowned hotels for African Americans in the Southeast. Postcards even promoted it as "America's Finest Colored Hotel." In addition to its fine accommodations, the Biltmore Hotel had a drugstore and a grill on the bottom floor. For over thirty years, famous African American visitors to the hotel could be found eating at the Biltmore Hotel Grill. It closed sometime in the 1960s, and the entire hotel was demolished in 1977, yet another victim of urban renewal.

In the 1950s, motels, which focus on providing lodging to automobile travelers, began to appear, and many also offered dining. Among these motels were chains, such as Howard Johnson's and Holiday Inn. In the 1960s, a traveler could dine at the General Sherman Restaurant in the General

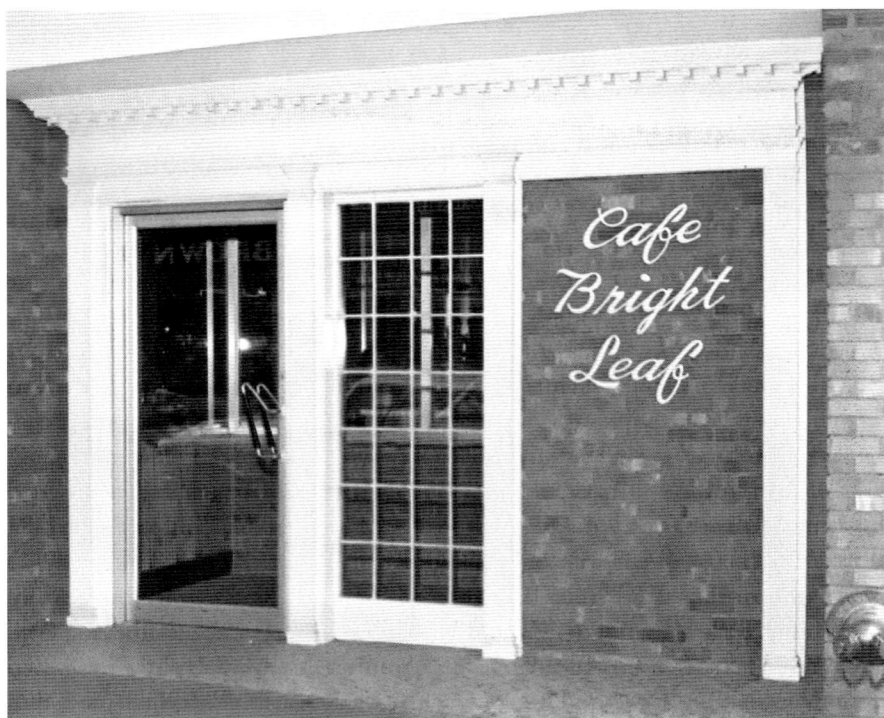

This page: The entrance and dining room of Café Bright Leaf at the Jack Tar Hotel (formerly the Washington Duke Hotel) in 1961. *Photo by Charles Cooper. Courtesy of the Durham Herald Collection, University of North Carolina–Chapel Hill.*

Joseph E. Johnston Motel. Located just west of town, at the intersection of Interstate 85 and Highway 70, the motels played off the fame of nearby Bennett Place, where Johnston's surrender brought the Civil War to a close. The Holiday Inn at 605 West Chapel Hill Street, which was built in 1959, went beyond just drawing transient visitors to Durham. Its Festa Room was a popular destination for Italian cuisine among locals in the 1960s. Postcards for the restaurant even carried the slogan, "Dining by candlelight and the sounds of far-away music in a romantic atmosphere." The Statler Hilton Inn, at 2424 Erwin Road, opened in 1966. Promoted as a luxury motor inn, the Statler Hilton offered dining and a swimming pool on its rooftop. Due to its location, the hotel was a popular lodging and dining location for visitors to Duke, and it was a popular lunch spot for employees of the Veterans Affairs and Duke hospitals. By the 1980s, the Statler Hilton had become the Brownstone Inn; it was demolished in the early 2000s and replaced by an office building.

A true luxury hotel finally returned to Durham in 1983, when the Sheraton University Center opened on Morrenne Road. The center offered guests two restaurant options: Praline's for more casual meals and Oliver's for fine dining. Advertisements promoted Praline's "southern-style charm," and Oliver's continental cuisine. In the mid-1980s, Oliver's offered students a five-course meal and live jazz for Valentine's Day in the *Duke Chronicle*. The advertisement stated, "It's an occasion for pleasure. Fine continental cuisine in comfortable surroundings."

For a few years—before Magnolia Grill and Fairview at the Washington Duke Inn opened—Oliver's was legitimately the pinnacle of traditional fine dining in Durham. It was the place to dine for well-heeled visitors to the city and nearby Duke University, as well as local residents. Among the top chefs to spend time in Oliver's kitchen was Cory Mattson, who apprenticed there in 1985 while he was a student at the Culinary Institute of America. Mattson then spent over two decades leading the kitchen at the highly acclaimed Fearrington House outside of Chapel Hill. The Sheraton University Center was acquired by Regal Hotels in 1996 and became the Millennium Hotel in 2001.

A high-end hotel finally returned to downtown when the Omni on East Chapel Hill Street opened in 1988. However, instead of building on the vacant site of the Washington Duke, most of the downtown block was torn down to make room for the new hotel. One of the buildings lost was the original home of Amos 'n' Andy hotdogs. The Omni offered dining, though it was primarily aimed at those staying in the hotel or visiting the

Above and opposite: The Jack Tar Hotel (formerly the Washington Duke Hotel) kitchen and staff in 1961. *Photo by Charles Cooper. Courtesy of the Durham Herald Collection, University of North Carolina–Chapel Hill.*

adjoining civic center. The Omni became the Marriott in the early 2000s. The Hilton at 3800 Hillsborough Road also opened in 1988. It contained a quality restaurant called Tipton's but was perhaps best known for its Blue Chips Lounge. The Duke University–owned Washington Duke Inn and Golf Course opened in 1988 as well. It's restaurant, Fairview, set a new standard for hotel dining in Durham and has remained one of the city's finest restaurants for over thirty years.

Today, hotel dining in Durham has seen a resurgence in popularity. With the rebirth of downtown, more hotels have come back and are once again destinations for more than just lodging. The Durham Hotel, a former bank at 315 East Chapel Hill Street, has a restaurant and rooftop bar run by James Beard Award–winning chef Andrea Reusing. Across the street, the long-vacant Jack Tar Motor Lodge, which was once connected by an overhead walkway to the original Washington Duke Hotel, has been reborn as Unscripted Durham. It offers several dining options, including one on its rooftop. The bottom floor houses Jack Tar and the Colonel's Daughter, a diner run by Gray Brooks, a veteran of downtown establishments like Pizzeria Toro and Littler, as well as a branch of Raleigh's popular Neomonde Mediterranean.

THE
FESTA ROOM
Open 7 days a week—5-12 p.m.

Festa Room Specials:
Served from 5-7 Sunday thru Thursday

1. **Spaghetti with meat sauce,**
Italian Bread, tossed salad
$1.25

2. **Baked lasagna,**
Tossed salad and Italian bread
$1.30

3. **Half-pound Charcoal-broiled Chopped Sirloin Steak**
With mushroom sauce, french fries, tossed salad and Italian bread **$1.35**

4. **14" Plain Pizza with tossed salad**
$1.00

Other Italian Specialties

Festa Room & Charcoal Hearth
RESTAURANT
605 WEST CHAPEL HILL ST., DOWNTOWN-DURHAM
AT HOLIDAY INN
EXCELLENT BANQUET FACILITIES 15-TO-250

Left: A 1966 advertisement for the Holiday Inn's Festa Room that appeared in the *Duke Chronicle*.

Below: Praline's (*shown here*) was the casual dining option of the Sheraton University Center. It served three meals and was known for its breakfast and lunch buffets, while the highly-regarded Oliver's only served dinner. *Photo by Jim Sparks. Courtesy of the Durham Herald Collection, University of North Carolina–Chapel Hill.*

Opposite: Chefs Frank Melgreen and Allen Slatky of Oliver's at the Sheraton University Center in 1982. *Photo by Jim Sparks. Courtesy of the Durham Herald Collection, University of North Carolina– Chapel Hill.*

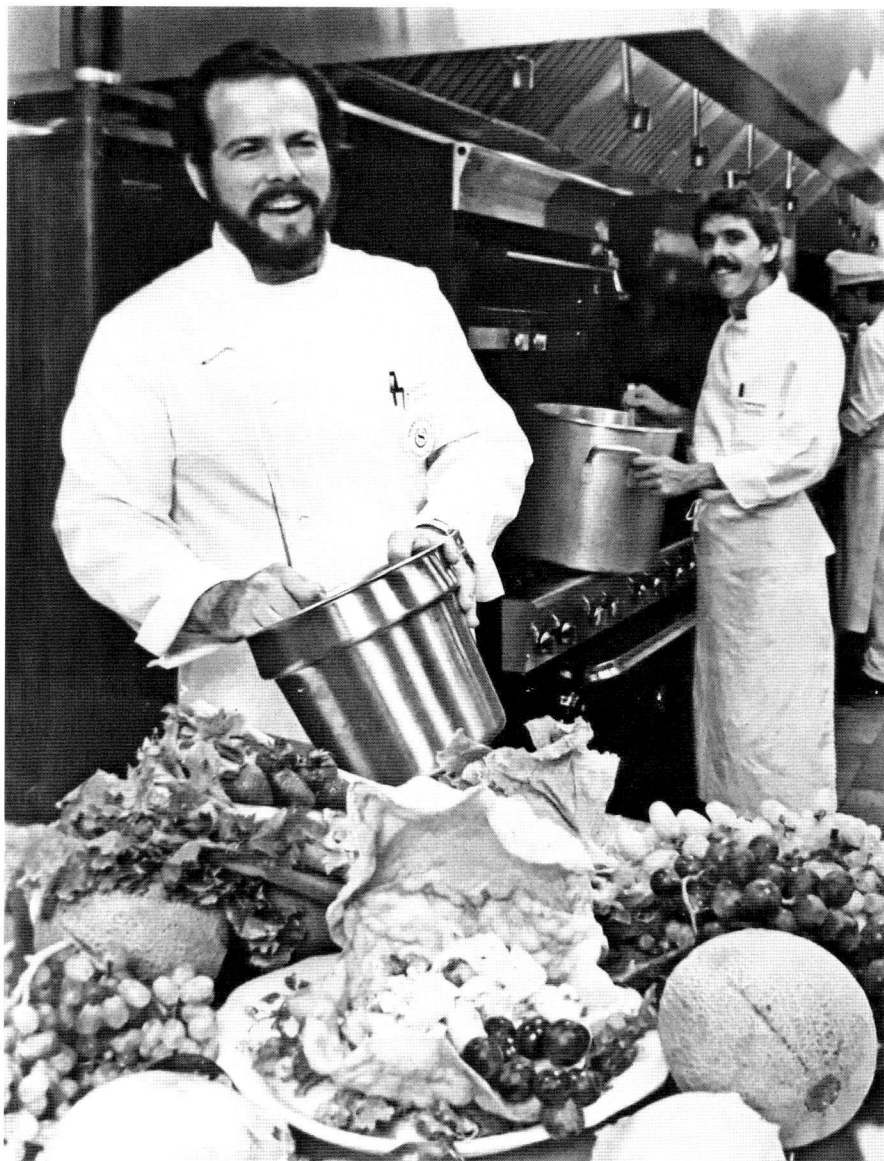

When the vacant Hill Building (commonly known as the former Central Carolina Bank and Suntrust Building) at 111 North Corcoran Street was reborn as 21c Museum Hotel, it also had a high-end restaurant. Named the Counting House—a play on the building's long bank history—the restaurant opened in 2015. The official press release stated, "Counting

Built in 1968 on the site of the former Center Theater, the Home Savings Bank building was an iconic representsation of mid-century design in downtown. In 2015, it was transformed into a fifty-three-room boutique hotel named the Durham. It features a top-level restaurant led by a James Beard Award–winning chef. *Photo by Chris Holaday.*

House offers a global perspective on regional dishes, with a menu celebrating North Carolina's rich heritage of fresh seafood, locally sourced seasonal ingredients and a strong emphasis on rotisserie and roasting techniques." It is interesting how cuisine that is associated with the words like "southern" and "local" has become so desirable, whereas only a couple decades ago, having classic Continental dishes on the menu was requisite for fine hotel restaurants.

6.

The Icons

A dining establishment that is able to survive the many challenges of the restaurant industry for twenty-five years has definitely found its place. These fifty restaurants—from small lunch cafés to white tablecloth fine-dining establishments—have all played an important role in shaping Durham's restaurant scene. Most of them have made it to their silver anniversary, and we rounded out the list with a few long-term establishments that have filled a niche in the city's food culture.

Any rating system or grouping would lead to a debate, as diners have always had their favorites. There will be dispute over why we mentioned one restaurant and not another, but the omission of any restaurant from this book is not intentional; we simply chose the restaurants that we thought best represented Durham's culinary history. In addition, some of the restaurants we have decided to include have been gone for years, while others were still open as of this book's publication date. That being said, we did not intend for this book to be an advertisement for these establishments; it is merely an assessment of what these restaurants have brought to the city.

ANNAMARIA'S PIZZA HOUSE
107 ALBEMARLE STREET

Today, pizza is viewed as an essential part of any college student's existence, but in the 1950s, it was essentially a foreign food in the South. In 1958, however, the first pizza restaurant in Durham, Annamaria's, was opened by New Jersey natives Bartholamew (Bat) and Annamaria Malanga.

Annamaria Malanga worked at Duke's Dope Shop, a soda fountain on campus, and got to know many of the school's students. The students from up north, who were familiar with pizza, began asking her to make it for them due to her Italian heritage. The student who got the most credit for launching Annamaria's, however, was star quarterback Sonny Jurgenson; he reportedly pestered Annamaria to make him pizza. She made the pizza, word spread and Annamaria was soon serving Duke students pizza from her home (which was on what is now Clarendon Street). Before long, the Malangas decided to open an official restaurant in a former family home on Albemarle Street.

The big personality of Bat Malanga, which often caused him to break out into song in the restaurant, led many patrons to simply refer to the establishment as Bat's. Regardless of what the restaurant was called,

Annamaria's, also known as Bat's. *Courtesy of the Durham County Library, North Carolina Collection.*

it was beloved by Duke students. In addition to pizza, Annamaria's became known for its spaghetti (referred to as spags and balls) and sub sandwiches. Most importantly, Annamaria's food was affordable for students. Its thirteen tables were crowded for twenty-eight years, and its customers paid at the register on the honor system. To occupy the crowds that were waiting for orders, the Malangas came up with a novel idea: stacks of comic books. Though it closed in 1986, Annamaria's is still fondly remembered by those who loved its comic books and Bat's singing as much as its pizza and spaghetti.

ANOTHERTHYME
109 NORTH GREGSON STREET

Mary Bacon. *Photo by Bernard Thomas. Courtesy of the Durham Herald Collection, University of North Carolina–Chapel Hill.*

With something of a hippie vibe, Somethyme was one of the earliest natural food restaurants in North Carolina. It opened on Broad Street in 1973 and flourished through the 1970s. In 1982, however, owner Mary Bacon decided to pursue a new venture and opened Anotherthyme near the newly developed Brightleaf Square. She combined the three bays of the building that had once housed Mayola's Grill into a single restaurant space.

Anotherthyme retained some of what its predecessor had offered, but it was a bit more upscale. Its menu also had a creativity that had not been seen before in Durham. The history section of Anotherthyme's website states the restaurant's mission: "With a philosophy of food that is based on rethinking seafood and vegetarian dishes as not being secondary to the meat and potatoes thing, Mary has spent years developing foods that are full of flavor and visually appealing without being dependent on a kitchen full of beef and chicken stock, heavy cream sauces or animal fats." Anotherthyme remained vegetarian until 1990, when Mary Bacon created her now-famous "AT Fried Chicken." The dish was followed by other meat offerings that were just as creative.

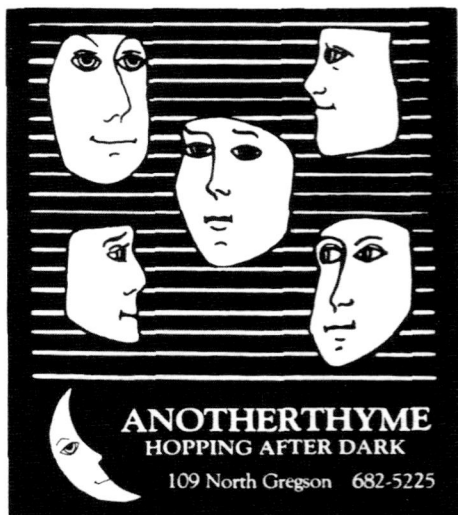

Anotherthyme advertisement from the *Duke Chronicle* in 1984. *Collection of the author.*

While Magnolia Grill is often credited with launching big changes in the Durham dining scene, Anotherthyme was really the forerunner of the food renaissance in the city. It and Mary Bacon introduced Durhamites to new flavors and showed them how much potential food can have. Anotherthyme was also the location of countless first dates, celebrations and special nights out. When it closed in October 2009, it left shoes that were impossible to fill. Don Ball had this to say about the restaurant:

> *The wonderful thing about Anotherthyme was that the menu stayed available a little later than a lot of restaurants kept their kitchens open. And it was a place where the industry folks went after they ended their shifts at other restaurants to come have a cocktail. They had great personalities behind the bar, and Mary's food was just absolutely delicious, but it had a quirkiness and a funkiness and a homeness that was just very comfortable.*

BAHN'S CUISINE
750 NINTH STREET

When it opened in 1988, Bahn's was essentially an inconspicuous hole-in-the-wall that few would have predicted to be a success over thirty years after its opening. Bahn's was perhaps the first restaurant in the city to offer true

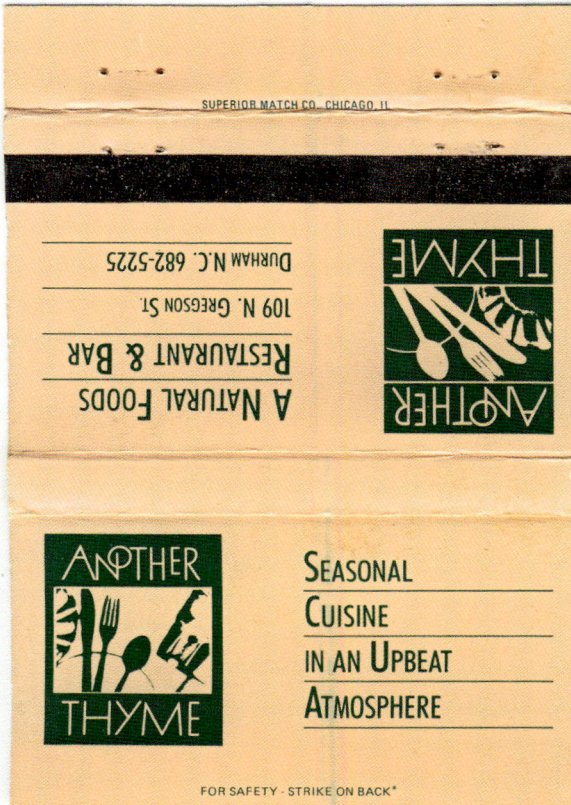

SUPERIOR MATCH CO., CHICAGO, IL

THYME

ANOTHER

A NATURAL FOODS
RESTAURANT & BAR

109 N. GREGSON ST.
DURHAM N.C. 682-5225

ANOTHER
THYME

SEASONAL
CUISINE
IN AN UPBEAT
ATMOSPHERE

FOR SAFETY · STRIKE ON BACK*

Left: Beginning in the early 1980s, Anotherthyme was a leader in transforming Durham's dining scene. *Promotional matchbook from the collection of the author.*

Below: A 1940s postcard featuring the Little Acorn. *Collection of the author.*

LITTLE ACORN RESTAURANT
DURHAM, NORTH CAROLINA

LITTLE ACORN

Above: An advertisement for the Little Acorn from the 1951 Carolina League baseball guide. *Collection of the author.*

Right: Matchbook promoting Mayola's Chili House. *Collection of the author.*

Above: The original Dog House on Miami Boulevard in 1972. *Courtesy of Mike Martin.*

Left: Marcus "Papa Jack" Jackson came to Durham from Alabama in 1934. A well-known figure in the Hayti area, Papa Jack was the proprietor of several restaurants, including Papa Jack's Grill (*promotional matchbook shown here*), the Congo Grill and the Rainbow Grill on Fayetteville Street. *Collection of the author.*

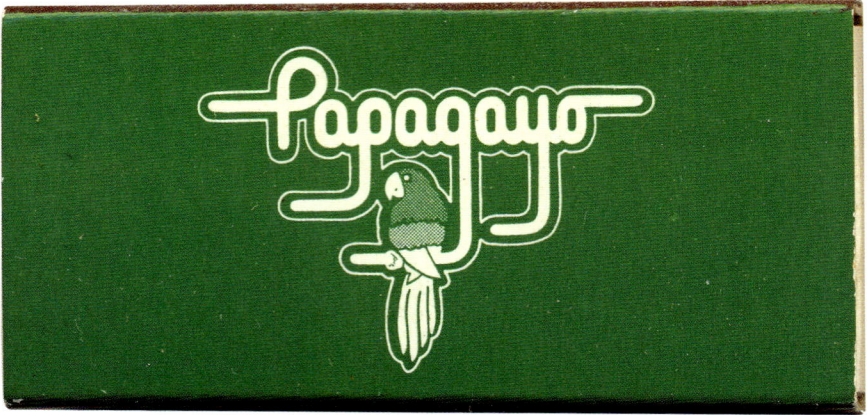

In the 1970s, Papagayo (*promotional matchbook shown here*) was one of the first restaurants in North Carolina to serve Mexican food. The first location was in Chapel Hill and the second, on Douglas Street just off Erwin, was in Durham. It later expanded to other locations in the state, including Wrightsville Beach and Kill Devil Hills. *Collection of the author.*

A 1983 Durham Bulls schedule featuring an ad for the Pizza Palace. *Collection of the author.*

A 1950s promotional matchbook from the Oriental. *Collection of the author.*

A menu from the Pizza Palace from the 1980s. *Collection of the author.*

Left: The building that has been home to Rue Cler since 2007 has housed many restaurants. This 1940s matchbook is from the R&M Café. It was followed by the C&W Café, the Mayflower Café and the Center Luncheonette. *Collection of the author.*

Right: The Sub Way invited patrons to "Eat a Big One" in this 1970s matchbook. *Collection of the author.*

The King's Sandwich Shop's building has changed little since the 1940s, and the takeout window remains crowded at lunchtime. *Photo by Chris Holaday.*

Customers wait for their orders outside La Vaquita, a popular taqueria on Chapel Hill Street. Run by Vera Cruz, Mexico natives Antonio Rodriguez, his wife, Elsa Guzman, and his brother Fidel Rodriguez for over a decade, the restaurant even garnered a mention in *Bon Appétit* magazine. *Photo by Chris Holaday.*

Chef Scott Howell, who has been responsible for several restaurants, including NanaSteak and Bar Virgile, shows off a dish at Nana's in 1993. *Photo by Peter Schumacher. Durham Herald Collection, University of North Carolina–Chapel Hill.*

Liberty Café in 1982. *Jerome Friar Photographic Collection, University of North Carolina–Chapel Hill.*

The interior of Parizäde is well known for its artwork and elaborate murals. *Photo by Bernard Thomas. Durham Herald Collection, University of North Carolina–Chapel Hill.*

A 1980s postcard promoting the Wabash Express Steak House. *Collection of the author.*

Elmo's has been one of the city's most popular breakfast destinations for over twenty years. The building was previously the home of the Ninth Street Bakery. *Photo by Chris Holaday.*

The Chicken Hut has been serving fried chicken out of its Fayetteville Street location for over fifty years. *Photo by Chris Holaday.*

BLUE LIGHT RESTAURANT

SPECIAL SANDWICHES		SANDWICHES		BEVERAGES		GIANT SODAS

SPECIAL SANDWICHES

DOUBLE BURGER 50
TWO PATTIES OF FRESHLY GROUND BEEF, MELTED CHEESE, PICKLE, LETTUCE

BLUE LIGHT FISHWICH 40
FRESH FISH FILLET ON TOASTED ROLL

STEAK SANDWICH 50
BIG TENDER BEEF STEAK, LETTUCE, TOMATO

BAKED HAM, LETTUCE, TOMATO . .50
A GREAT HAM SANDWICH

DOUBLE BURGER PLATTER 75
DOUBLE BURGER WITH FRENCH FRIES AND COLE SLAW

FISHWICH PLATTER 65
FISHWICH WITH FRENCH FRIES AND COLE SLAW

STEAK SANDWICH PLATTER 75
STEAK SANDWICH WITH FRENCH FRIES, COLE SLAW

BAKED HAM PLATTER 75
BAKED HAM WITH FRENCH FRIES AND COLE SLAW

SANDWICHES

Hamburgers 30
Cheeseburger 35
Hot Dog 30
Bar-B-Q 45
Bacon, Lettuce, Tomato .40
Toasted Cheese 25

COMPLETE PLATTERS

BAR B-Q PLATTER
CHOPPED BAR-B-Q — SERVED WITH FRENCH FRIES, COLE SLAW, BUTTERED ROLL
1.25

SHRIMP PLATTER
JUMBO FANTAIL SHRIMP WITH FRENCH FRIES, COLE SLAW, SHRIMP SAUCE, BUTTERED ROLL
1.35

CHICKEN PLATTER
½ CHICKEN, FRENCH FRIES, COLE SLAW, BUTTERED ROLL
1.35

FRENCH FRIES
.20

ONION RINGS
.35

BEVERAGES

SHAKES 25
MALTS — FRUITS 30
COCA COLA . . . .10 and .20
PEPSI COLA . . . .10 and .20
DIET PEPSI . . . .10 and .20
ORANGE ADE . . .10 and .20
MOUNTAIN DEW. .10 and .20
MILK 15
TEA 10
COFFEE 10
HOT CHOCOLATE 15

GIANT SODAS
.25 and .30

GREAT SUNDAES
.25 and .30

CARRY OUT ORDERS—PHONE US—
WE WILL HAVE IT READY TO GO

PHONE: 286-1211

PIZZA
CHEESE PIZZA 85   PEPPERONI PIZZA . . 1.00
MUSHROOM PIZZA . . 1.00   SAUSAGE PIZZA . . 1.00
COMBINATION PIZZA 1.25

A 1950s menu from the Blue Light. *Courtesy of John Boy.*

Foster's shortly after it opened in 1990. The building once housed a tractor and lawnmower dealer. *Photo by Biar Orrell. Durham Herald Collection, University of North Carolina–Chapel Hill.*

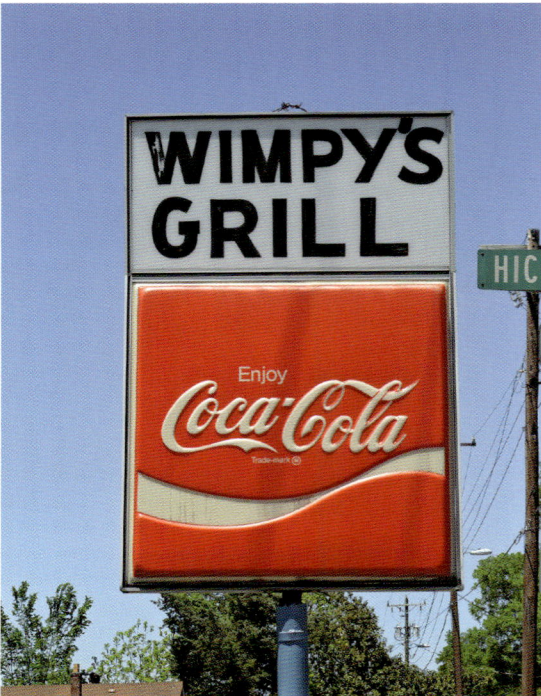

Above: For over half a century, Hartman's Steakhouse— shown here in 1993—was a popular destination for a night out. *Durham Herald Collection, University of North Carolina– Chapel Hill.*

Left: Wimpy's burgers and hotdogs attracted loyal followers for thirty-two years. Its sign went dark for good in April 2019. *Photo by Chris Holaday.*

Above: Pastry chef and co-owner of Magnolia Grill Karen Barker (*right*) shows off a creation with assistant Ivy Lewis in 1994. *Photo by Biar Orrell. Durham Herald Collection, University of North Carolina–Chapel Hill.*

Left: A Dillard's Barbeque menu from the early 2000s. *Courtesy of Wilma Dillard.*

At Durham establishments, from Amos 'N' Andy's, King's, the Dog House, tobacco warehouse cafés and many more, the Carolina-style hotdog has been an important part of the menu for decades. *Photo by Joshua Bousel.*

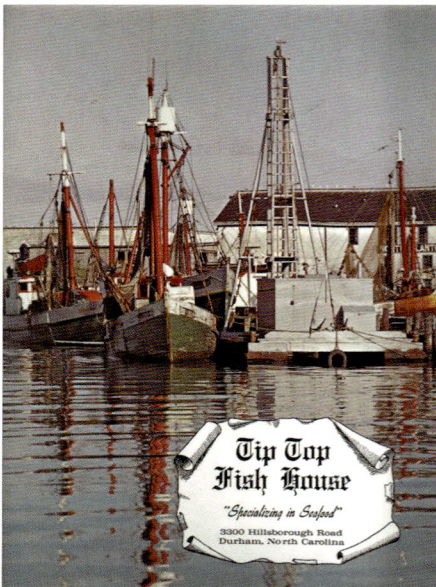

A 1970s menu for Tip-Top Fish House. *Courtesy of Belinda Watkins Rasmussen.*

"The Biltmore Hotel and Grill is home away from home for the colored tourist" reads the back of this 1930s postcard. In the age of segregation, the Biltmore Hotel on Pettigrew Street provided some of the finest accommodations for African Americans in the South. The popular grill was on the right side of the ground floor. *Collection of the author.*

The Malbourne Hotel, seen here in a 1920s postcard, was Durham's finest when it opened in 1912. It was a particularly popular spot for Sunday dinner in the early years. Though the Malbourne had declined in prestige, its coffee shop was still well-advertised as a dining destination fifty years later. *Collection of the author.*

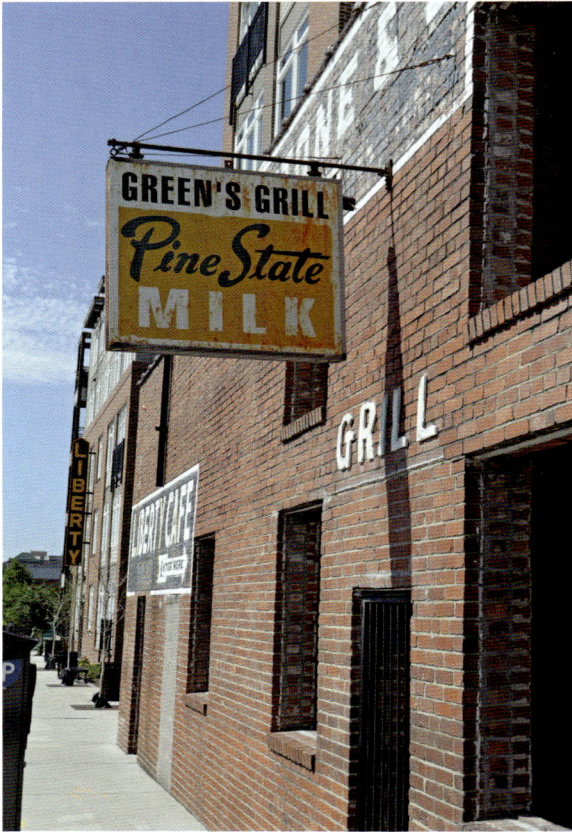

Left: Long after the last tobacco auction was held in 1984, Liberty Warehouse continued to house an assortment of businesses, as well as Green's Grill. In 2011, the warehouse suffered storm damage and was deemed impossible to repair. Though the building was replaced by a condominium complex, the façade was preserved as a tribute to its important past. *Photo by Chris Holaday.*

Below: When the nearly fifteen-acre American Tobacco complex was renovated for offices and restaurants in the early 2000s, many details of the historic building were preserved. One was the entrance to a small café, the Lunch Downstairs, which served the employees of the cigarette factory. *Photo by Chris Holaday.*

Vietnamese dishes, and it also offers Chinese favorites and a rotation of popular specials, including vegetarian Wednesdays and unique Vietnamese weekends. The economical menu offerings (which are served on disposable plates) have made the cash-only restaurant popular with two generations of Duke students. Only a few guests are lucky enough to dine in the restaurant, since its seating is very limited.

THE BLUE LIGHT
1605 ERWIN ROAD, AT THE INTERSECTION OF PETTIGREW

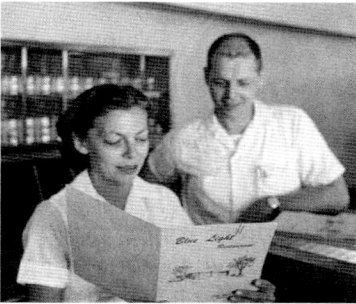

Waitress Ann Argenbright and owner Sam Boy at the Blue Light in 1961. *Courtesy of the Roland Giduz Photographic Collection, University of North Carolina–Chapel Hill.*

As a favorite hangout for Durham locals and Duke students for twenty-five years, the Blue Light has what is perhaps the most interesting history of any restaurant in the city. It all began in 1946, when Carl Boy and his sons Sam, Carl Jr. and James opened Boy's Esso Service Center. A family friend asked if they could open a hotdog stand next to the station; he did so, but soon lost interest in the business. The Boy brothers saw potential in the idea, however, and took the hotdog stand to the next level by constructing a full drive-in restaurant in 1949. Named the Blue Light, the restaurant became the place to be seen—or to perhaps show off a new car—for many young Durhamites in the 1950s and 1960s.

After his brothers moved away, Sam Boy took over the restaurant and ran it with his wife, Gerry, whom he married in 1950. The Esso station was closed and replaced with a car wash, and at one point, the Boys even operated a miniature golf course across the street. In the early 1970s, the area was changing; Duke University constructed student apartments at the nearby Central Campus. In order to serve that growing market, the Boys converted the Blue Light into a convenience store they called Sam's Quik Shop in 1974.

As the times changed, the store adapted. Along with selling gasoline, the store sold snacks, magazines, videos and numerous other items before

Blue Light Restaurant

Split Pea Soup	.25
Chef's Salad	.25
Shrimp Cocktail	.60

Below Entrees are Served with Two Vegetables, Bread & Beverage

1. Irish Beef Stew	1.00
2. Baked Sugar Cured Ham, Pineapple Ring	1.20
3. Brunswick Stew	1.00
4. Calf's Liver with Bacon Strip	1.20
5. Fried Shrimp or Scallops	1.25
6. Deviled Crab or Fried Perch	1.00
7. Roast Sirloin of Beef, Brown Gravy	1.20
8. Breaded Veal Steak, Brown Gravy	1.10
9. One Quarter Fry Chicken	1.00
10. Roast Fresh Ham with Brown Gravy	1.10

Vegetables Today   Choice of Two

String Beans	Turnip Green	Pickled beets
Creamed Corn	Black Eyed Peas	Potato Salad
Buttered Carrots	Creamed Potatoes	Fruit Jello
Pear Salad	Tossed Salad	Apple Sauce

Beverage   Coffee   or   Iced Tea

* *

Hot Roast Beef or Pork Sandwich with Potatoes	.85
Barbecue & Brunswick Stew Combination with Slaw	1.10
Homemade Pies	.20

Left: The Blue Light menu from the 1940s. *Courtesy of John Boy.*

Below: The exterior of the Blue Light, circa 1955. *Courtesy of John Boy.*

it settled on beer. "I credit my mother with making sure we had a good beer selection starting in the 1970s," said John Boy Jr., who took over the business in the late 1980s. "Videos and magazines eventually went down in sales but one thing that never did was beer. That's why we decided to focus on it." Sam's Quik Shop became a mecca for beer lovers, as it carried a huge selection of local craft beers and brews from around the world. A bar was even added to the station, so it could offer numerous beers on tap. In early 2019, Sam's Quik Shop closed and gave way to the development of an apartment building. Its legacy lives on, however, at Sam's Bottle Shop on Highway 54 behind Woodcroft Shopping Center. There, patrons can sip a beer in front of pictures of the original Blue Light restaurant.

BISCUIT KING
816 NINTH STREET

A blue-painted cinderblock building with a cartoon king brandishing a tray of biscuits painted on the front window was the ultimate breakfast destination for countless Durhamites for twenty-eight years. The Biscuit King's building was constructed in the early 1960s for a franchise of the barbecue restaurant Little Pigs of America. Based in Memphis, the chain grew quickly but filed bankruptcy in 1967. For a time, the space was home to a grill called 'Round the Clock, but in 1976, Earl Mize took over the building and opened Biscuit King there. In 1986, his daughter Bonny and her husband, Jerry Turner, bought the restaurant.

Located between Erwin Mill, Duke's East Campus and Watts Hospital, Biscuit King drew a diverse clientele. Mill workers and college students all came to sample Biscuit King's wide array of biscuits. Usually, around twenty different biscuits were offered at the restaurant, and they were served with fillings, including molasses, fatback and even grits. At lunchtime, diners could enjoy burgers, "sweetshot" sandwiches (fried chicken with honey) and barbecue, all under the watchful gaze of the Duke basketball players whose photos covered the walls. To add to Biscuit King's uniqueness, the Turners began to offer tomatoes from their garden in the summer, as well as homemade fried pies and individually wrapped slices of cheddar cheese.

Like so many other restaurants, Biscuit King fell victim to the redevelopment plans of its building's landlord. The restaurant closed for good at the end of February 2004. Biscuit King was not forgotten, however; in 2016, a tabletop-sized model of it was featured in the exhibit "Southern Accent: Seeking the American South in Contemporary Art" at Duke's Nasher Art Museum.

BULLOCK'S BARBECUE
3330 QUEBEC DRIVE

You can't have a southern city without a go-to barbecue restaurant. For over sixty years, Bullock's has served barbecue to the people of Durham. The restaurant can trace its beginning's back to Glen Bullock's backyard on South Alston Avenue. There, in the 1940s, he began cooking pigs and selling barbecue to his friends and neighbors (reportedly for thirty-five cents per pound). The demand for his barbecue eventually grew, so in 1952, he rented a building at 3601 Hillsborough Road in order to open a true restaurant. Glen's wife, Lillian, and his son, Tommy, helped run the business, and Tommy took it over in 1965. In 1970, the restaurant was still booming, so the Bullocks built a new building on land they owned and moved just over half a mile to the east.

Over the years, no visit to Durham was complete without a meal at Bullock's. Many celebrities even stopped by, and the restaurant's walls were soon filled with autographed photos of athletes, musicians and actors who had enjoyed the barbecue, Brunswick stew, fried chicken, slaw, beans, hushpuppies, collard greens and the wide range of desserts offered there.

Customers wait to be seated at Bullock's in 1988. *Photo by Jim Thornton. Courtesy of the Durham Herald Collection, University of North Carolina–Chapel Hill.*

Tommy Bullock stirs the Brunswick stew as his parents look on in 1978. *Photo by Harold Moore. Courtesy of the Durham Herald Collection, University of North Carolina–Chapel Hill.*

Tommy Bullock passed away in December 2018. His humble obituary in the *Herald Sun* simply stated, "Mr. Bullock loved to cook and especially loved seeing customers enjoying a good meal." Today, his family is continuing the restaurant's legacy, and a third generation of Bullocks is serving their family's famous barbecue and sides to Durham residents. Bullock's remains the oldest continuously operating restaurant in the city.

THE CHICKEN BOX, NOW THE CHICKEN HUT
410 SOUTH ROXBORO STREET (1956–1966),
3019 FAYETTEVILLE STREET

The Chicken Hut is the oldest African American–owned restaurant in Durham, and it is the second-oldest overall, just after Bullock's. The restaurant had its beginnings as a concession stand at the Michaux Drive-In Theater on Highway 55 at Riddle Road. Before long, owners Claiborne

An advertisement for the Chicken Box from *Hill's 1962 Durham City Guide. Courtesy of Digital NC.*

Tapp Jr. and his sister, Julia Tapp, decided to open another location in Hayti, a part of town that had a potentially larger clientele pool. The pair called their restaurant the Chicken Box and opened its doors on Pine Street (now Roxboro Street) in 1957.

In 1966, urban renewal forced the Chicken Box and many of its neighbors out of their Hayti locations. The city offered to relocate the restaurant to Tin City, a building that housed displaced African American–owned businesses under one roof. Instead, the Tapps decided to buy land a few blocks south of North Carolina Central University on Fayetteville Street, where they rebuilt their restaurant from the ground up. With the new location came a slightly new name: the Chicken Hut.

Peggy Johnson was in high school when she began working as a carhop at the Chicken Box's original Durham location, at the corner of NC-55 and Riddle Road, in 1957. After spending a year at college, Johnson returned to work at the Chicken Box. She eventually married Claiborne Tapp and helped grow the business. At one point, the Tapps had five Chicken Huts in Durham and Chapel Hill, but poor health forced Claiborne Sr. to downsize to just the flagship location. When he died in 1998, Peggy Tapp continued running the restaurant with help from her sisters, Ruth Dash and JoAnn Johnson. When Peggy passed away in 2018, her son Tre took over as proprietor. Today, he continues the family tradition of serving Durham's most famous fried chicken. Mel Melton had this to say about the Chicken Hut:

> I loved the Chicken Hut back in the 80s. You ordered fried chicken on one side, and the other side was cafeteria-style. But the fried chicken was it; it wasn't sitting around—they made it to order. I went there just for the fried chicken, and I will always remember Miss Peggy. She was wonderful.

COLLEGE INN
1306 FAYETTEVILLE STREET

In 1933, William H. "Bill" Jones, a recent graduate from Greensboro's North Carolina A&T, moved to Durham and opened the College Inn just up Fayetteville Street from what is now North Carolina Central University. The College Inn's tasty-yet-affordable barbeque, fried chicken and chili hotdogs were popular with students. The restaurant was also the source of Budweiser kegs for many of the university's fraternity parties, and it even hosted the reception for the first graduating class of the university's law school. The College Inn always had a close relationship with the student population, and its owner, Bill Jones, reportedly even offered to pay the tuition of some students who were in financial need. He also sponsored a local baseball team called the College Inn Rangers.

During the days of segregation, the College Inn was often a destination for visiting African American entertainers and celebrities; stars like bandleader Duke Ellington even dined there. After Jones's death in 1959, his wife, Martha, continued the restaurant's tradition of community involvement and bought the neighboring Page General Store in an attempt to preserve it. The College Inn finally closed in the late 1980s, and its building now houses an African and soul food restaurant called New Visions of Africa, which opened in 2004.

COSMIC CANTINA
1920 PERRY STREET

Tucked away in a second-floor location just off Ninth Street, one can find a restaurant serving "the best Mexican food on the planet"—at least according to the building's sign. Cosmic Cantina has been an inexpensive late-night favorite of Duke students since 1995. It was founded by Duke students Cosmos Lyles, who was studying engineering and physics at the time, and Sterling Lanier, who was an English and history major. Having both grown up in California, the fraternity brothers were familiar with the numerous burrito restaurants that were so common on the West Coast. They realized that these were missing from the market in Durham, and the dining options were very limited for Duke students who wanted to eat late at night.

Doing much of the work themselves, the partners and friends saved money and renovated what had once been a carpet remnants store. The Cosmic Cantina, which was within walking distance of Duke's East Campus, opened just as the fall semester of 1995 began. It offered large California-style burritos filled with fresh, organic ingredients, along with beer and margaritas. Perhaps most important to the university's students, the Cosmic Cantina's prices were low, and the establishment remained open until 4:00 a.m.

Lanier left the business after a year, but Lyles continued to run the restaurant. He eventually opened a second location in Chapel Hill to serve University of North Carolina students, and he later took a bolder step and opened a third Cosmic Cantina in New York City (which has since closed). By sticking to its original goal for well over two decades, the Cosmic Cantina certainly found its niche in Durham's dining market. And it isn't a restaurant that has slipped off the radar; in its annual Eat and Drink awards in 2019, *Indy Week* named the Cosmic Cantina's burritos the best in Durham County.

DEVINE'S
904 WEST MAIN

In 1975, Gene Devine, a native of Massachusetts and former Blue Devil football player, decided that there was no better way to stay involved with Durham and Duke sports fans than to open a sports bar and grill. Devine chose a location on Main Street, across from the yet-to-be-renovated Brightleaf Square, that had been home to several different bars and restaurants (including one called Maxwell's) over the years. Devine's opened in 1978, and it has remained a constant in the area, which has seen a lot of change. With a good beer selection, various sporting events playing on the television and a menu full of what could be called good American bar staples (burgers, wings and sandwiches), Devine's has found its niche in Durham's food scene.

BLUE DEVIL DINING

The students at Duke University have long had close relationships with many of Durham's iconic restaurants. Their patronage has led to the success of many restaurants, and many of the restaurants around Durham have made a point to advertise in the student newspaper, the *Duke Chronicle*. Former students, even those who reside far from Durham today, still have vivid memories of dining in the city.

Parkers was far and away my best food memory from Durham. It was my first real adventure off campus when I first got there in the mid-1980s. Going to Parker's was great because it enabled me to forget about the pressures of being at Duke and really enabled me to connect with the city of Durham. Going to Parker's and a Bulls game was a really great night out. Anotherthyme had the best atmosphere in Durham. It was the place to take a date to really impress her. There were always a few things on the menu that seemed, to my young self, really sophisticated to order. Plus, they really supported live jazz for a long time, so it was fun to go there just for that.

—Mike Howell

The Ivy Room was really it, and it was the place to go in Durham in 1972, when I started at Duke. It was cheap enough for students to frequent often. Chipped beef on toast kind of everyman food. Saddle and Fox was the upscale venue that was for special occasions. I went there three or four times as a student in the 1970s. It was very good but not cheap enough for the average joe, and it had a kitschiness, as its name suggests.

—Chris Sutch

When I first came to Durham to go to Duke in 1988, the idea was that if you wanted to go out and do anything, you had to go to Chapel Hill. Among the first things that I remember doing off campus was dining at Anotherthyme. It wasn't vegetarian, but it had vegetarian options. It had a really interesting and unusual mix of things on the menu. Since I was a student, that was a place I went with my parents. There weren't a lot of places that I could afford to go on my own—that I knew of at least. El Rodeo in Brightleaf Square, that was an early one. We went there a fair amount. It was inexpensive and good. The food courts at both Northgate and South Square Malls. There was a place called Spinnakers at South Square; that was, like, a nicer place to go as a student. It wouldn't break the bank. They had funny little things they would do, like bring you bread baked in a terra-cotta flowerpot. Bahn's was another one we would go to on Ninth Street.

I don't think anything has changed there since. You could get a full plate of food for a little over two dollars. And there was Broad Street Café, but I don't think I went east of Bright Leaf Square the whole time I was there. The prevailing notion was that there was nothing beyond Bright Leaf; it was sort of a demarcation. We really focused on the malls and Ninth Street. That was all we knew in terms of off campus as Duke students at that time.

—Gary Kueber

DILLARD'S BARBECUE
3921 FAYETTEVILLE STREET

For nearly sixty years, Durham's barbecue scene was dominated by Bullock's and Dillard's. In 1953, a year after what would be his cross-town competition opened, Samuel Dillard opened his own barbecue restaurant. With $85 of his own money and a $1,000 loan, the Mississippi native originally opened a grocery store, but a friend of his convinced him that a restaurant would be more successful. That friend taught Dillard how to slow-cook hogs, thus Dillard's Barbecue was born. Dillard and his wife, Geneva, ran the cafeteria-style eatery, which soon became famous for its barbecue, ribs and unique offerings that included its popular carrot soufflé. By the 1990s, it was serving 1,600 pounds of pork barbecue per week.

In North Carolina, there has long been a debate over which sauce is better—the vinegar-based Eastern-style sauce or the Lexington-style sauces, which incorporate ketchup. Dillard's went its own way, however, and used a South Carolina–style mustard-based sauce. It set them apart, and it led to the development of a side business of bottling and selling the unique sauce, which is still available today.

For a long time, the message board on the bottom of the restaurant's sign simply read: "Deuteronomy 8:3." Containing the statement "man does not live on bread alone," the Bible verse was a testament to the owner's religious convictions.

Dillard's may be gone, but its famous sauce is still available. *Courtesy of Wilma Dillard.*

The restaurant was always a family affair; four of Sam Dillard's sons, his daughter and his grandchildren worked there. In 1997, after he passed away, his daughter, Wilma, took over the famed barbecue joint. Citing a downturn in the economy, the restaurant—by far the oldest African American–owned dining establishment in the city—announced that it would close in March 2011. The restaurant's patrons were not the only ones who bemoaned its loss; for nearly thirty years, Dillard's had also been the official purveyor of barbecue for the countless baseball fans at Durham Bulls games.

THE DOG HOUSE

With a distinctive building that resembles an actual doghouse and trashcans shaped like fire hydrants, the Dog House has been a familiar sight in Durham for nearly fifty years. In 1970, Stuart Henderson, who had been running his own metal fabrication company in Durham, decided to follow a different career path and opened a restaurant. Using family recipes for chili, slaw and stew, he opened his first Dog House location on Miami Boulevard. For his restaurant, Henderson created hotdog variations that were each named after a type of dog, such as the Collie Dog, Boxer Dog and the Ol' Yallow, which was covered in hot Velveeta-type cheese. The hotdogs proved to be very popular, and other locations were soon opened around town. Stuart Henderson passed away in 2010, but his wife, Charlotte, and his daughters, Jessica Isaacs and Joan Henderson, continued to run the chain, which shrunk from ten locations to five—four in Durham and one in Hillsborough.

In 2015, Mike Martin, a research chemist who had recently lost his job at Research Triangle Park, was looking for a new career opportunity. He had often eaten hotdogs from a nearby Dog House location, so on a whim, he emailed the Henderson family and asked if they would be interested in selling the business. The answer was yes, and Martin took over. He soon took on his partners: Shetal Desai, a long-time employee of the Dog House, and her husband, Amish. The company began offering franchise opportunities, and the first was located in Greenville, North Carolina. Not surprisingly, the owner of the franchise is a Durham native who grew up eating hotdogs at the Dog House.

ELMO'S
776 NINTH STREET

If the waiting lines on Saturday mornings are any indication, Elmo's has mastered the art of breakfast. Warm and inviting with an old-fashioned diner atmosphere, it has been an important part of the Durham community for over twenty years. Elmo's famous breakfast is served all day, but the menu also offers burgers, sandwiches and a wide assortment of other dishes. In fact, Elmo's fare is so well known that it was even featured on Rachel Ray's *$40 a Day* show on the Food Network in 2004.

The first Elmo's opened in Carrboro, but the owners had so many customers coming from Durham that they decided to open a second location. In the spring of 1997, in a space that was formerly occupied by Ninth Street Bakery, Elmo's served its first breakfast in the city. Diners with close community ties have long been a part of Durham's restaurant scene, and today, co-owners Cammie Brantley; her husband, Wayne Hodges; and Amy Testa continue that tradition.

EL RODEO
905 WEST MAIN STREET, BRIGHTLEAF SQUARE

In the late 1980s, Mexican food was thought of as a somewhat gourmet cuisine in Durham. As the city's demographics changed and more people with Mexican heritage moved in, the market for everyday Mexican food grew. During the first week of 1989, El Rodeo opened at Brightleaf Square in a location that was formerly home to Swenson's and an English pub called the Duke of York. El Rodeo provided a wide range of dishes that were economical as well as authentic. It also offered dishes that had been somewhat adapted to American tastes (in other words, less spicy), which widened its appeal. While El Rodeo might be considered a server of rather commonplace Mexican food today, it exposed a new generation of customers to what Mexican cuisine had to offer.

The El Rodeo at Brightleaf was the first of the several restaurants in North Carolina to bear the name. It is often considered to be a chain, but it is really more like a restaurant co-op. According to the official website, "The truth of the matter is that they are more like individual families from Jalisco, Mexico, at each location. This is why they are not exactly alike. Even though we do work together [to make] them similar." Regardless, El Rodeo has had an important impact on Durham's restaurant landscape for thirty years.

FAIRVIEW RESTAURANT
WASHINGTON DUKE INN & GOLF CLUB
3001 CAMERON BOULEVARD

For over thirty years, Fairview has quietly remained the peak of fine dining in Durham, perhaps because it is located in a hotel; however, it does not draw the same hype as some of the other dining locations in the city.

Named after the one-time Duke family mansion in downtown Durham, Fairview opened in the fall of 1988 in the new Duke University–owned Washington Duke Inn. The Washington Duke Inn was created to serve the university while attracting the same clientele as the city's other top hotels (Omni, Hilton and Sheraton). The inn provided a more complete experience by offering luxury lodging and dining, as well as a top-level golf course.

When it opened, the Fairview and adjoining Bull Durham bar offered seating for 120 people. In a preview of the opening in the *Duke Chronicle*, the newspaper stated, "The restaurant will feature popular regional cooking such as barbecue and southern cuisine, as well as continental cuisine." It went on to note that the restaurant's chef, who had been hired from the Chapel Hill Country Club, would offer specialties such as "rack of lamb, Veal Forestier

The Fairview dining room at the Washington Duke Inn set up for a Christmas banquet. *Photograph by Chris Holaday.*

and several fresh seafood dishes." In the 1980s, before Southern cuisine truly came into its own, a restaurant could not be considered "fancy" if it didn't offer a few classic French dishes.

Today, Fairview is a cutting-edge, modern restaurant led by a chef who specializes in creating dishes that use North Carolina ingredients. It is one of only two restaurants in North Carolina to garner both the AAA Four Diamond and the Forbes Travel Guide Four-Star awards. In addition, it received the *Wine Spectator* Award of Excellence. Fairview is also famous for its brunches, but it's perhaps equally famous for its view of the golf course, which is unrivaled by any restaurant in the city.

FISHMONGERS
806 WEST MAIN STREET

With a neon sign that brightly announced, "OYSTER BAR," Fishmongers Seafood Market Crab and Oyster House was the place to go for seafood in the downtown area for over thirty years. Located in a building that was originally a Cadillac dealership in the 1920s and a Plymouth dealership for

Fishmongers in 1991. *Photo by Jim Thornton. Courtesy of the Durham Herald Collection, University of North Carolina–Chapel Hill.*

many years, Fishmongers was opened by Gary Bass in 1983. As a restaurant that was something between a casual eatery and a grungy dive—and with a famously funky smell—Fishmongers was loved by some and avoided by others. Either way, it thrived for thirty-two years with its menu of shrimp, oysters and fried fish of many types. Its market offered everything from live lobsters to swordfish. Unfortunately, it all came to something of an ignominious end in November 2015, when the Department of Revenue seized the business and changed the building's locks due to tax issues.

In 2017, Matt Kelly, the distinguished chef responsible for a considerable amount of the restaurant growth in downtown Durham over the last few years (Mateo Bar de Tapas, Mothers & Sons Trattoria and Lucky's Delicatessen), opened Saint James Seafood in the old Fishmongers location. The new restaurant is definitely more upscale than its predecessor; gone are the brown butcher paper–covered picnic tables, the brick building is now painted white and blue, but Fishmongers' checkerboard floor remains.

FOSTER'S MARKET
2694 CHAPEL HILL BOULEVARD

Even the restaurant's official website acknowledges that Foster's is hard to describe. Its self-description says that Foster's is a "restaurant, coffee bar, specialty food store and catering company." Whatever one wants to call it, Foster's has been a culinary phenomenon since 1990. It is a popular gathering spot, especially for lunch and weekend brunch. Every weekend, one can find Foster's random assortment of chairs and tables on its lawn and in other outdoor areas filled with an assortment of Duke students, their parents, locals and plenty of dogs.

Sara Foster, a native of Tennessee, attended culinary school in New York before landing a job as a catering chef for Martha Stewart in Connecticut. She eventually decided to open her own restaurant, and she and her husband, Peter Sellers, moved to Durham to open Foster's Market. The market became such a success that Foster opened a second location in Chapel Hill in 1998, which she sold after fifteen years. Over the years, Foster's Market has won many awards, from *Indy Week*'s "Best Lunch Spot in the Triangle" to "2010 Restaurateur of the Year" from the North Carolina Restaurant and Lodging Association. In addition, Sara Foster has authored six cookbooks, contributed to *Martha Stewart Living* and other magazines and she has been a guest on radio and television shows.

THE GREEN CANDLE
542 EAST PETTIGREW STREET

In 1953, with help from her mother and sisters, Azona Allen opened the Green Candle in a Pettigrew Street location that had previously been a beauty salon. With food that likely reminded its owners of home, the small restaurant soon became popular with students from nearby North Carolina Central University (then called North Carolina College). A discount was even offered to students on lunches, and a meatloaf dinner was available for the princely sum of fifty-two cents. The Green Candle's ad in the 1958 Durham city guide stated: "We serve one meal a day, but it's the best in Hayti."

In the age of segregation, African American celebrities who were visiting Durham sought out the Green Candle, partly because they were welcome and partly because they wanted some of Azona Allen's famed cooking. Ike and Tina Turner even reportedly dined there in the 1960s. But Allen was not star-struck by her famous diners; when James Brown came into the restaurant late after one of his concerts, she told him that service was over with no exceptions. Even later, the Green Candle

Azona Allen at work in the kitchen of the Green Candle in 1971. *Photo by Harold Moore. Courtesy of the Durham Herald Collection, University of North Carolina–Chapel Hill.*

maintained a reputation that went beyond its neighborhood, and Duke (and later NBA) basketball star Grant Hill was a big fan.

Like many businesses in Hayti, the Green Candle lost its Pettigrew Street location due to the city's infamous urban renewal plan. The city built the "Tin City" facility on Fayetteville Street for displaced businesses, and Allen moved her restaurant there. She later moved to the nearby Phoenix Square shopping center, where the Green Candle remained until 1998, when Allen decided to retire and close the business at the age of eighty-one. In 2001, she was presented with the key to the city by mayor pro tem Howard Clement for her long service to the community.

> *I will always remember Ms. Azona Allen and the Green Candle restaurant in Phoenix Square. Ms. Allen, by the time I met her, was the only one cooking, and she would walk across the street to the Winn Dixie that was located in Heritage Square to bring fresh vegetables to cook daily for the hungry crowd. She made some of the best oven-fried chicken that I had ever tasted in my life. She also had great meatloaf and iced tea that was so good and so sweet that I call it, today, "diabetes in a cup," but I would pay anything to relive the memories!*
>
> —*Andre Vann*

HARTMAN'S STEAK HOUSE
1703 EAST GEER STREET

Located on the far eastern edge of town, not far from the Starlite Drive-In Theater, Hartman's Steak House was something of a destination dining experience; people would travel to town to go to dinner before going to see a movie. Hartman's was one of those places where people went to celebrate or to impress a date. Even in its later years, after the city had grown and changed, Hartman's remined a time capsule to the past, with its fireplace, wood-paneled interior covered by stapled business cards and view over the pond in the back. One could easily imagine that they had been transported back to the 1950s as they enjoyed Hartman's famous friend banana peppers, blue cheese salad, liver with onions and, of course, steak.

In 1941, Charles "Pop" Hartman and his wife, Gertrude, opened Hartman's Grill and Tavern. By the late 1950s, they had remodeled and added on to the building. The restaurant's name was also changed to reflect its new focus on steaks. Pop Hartman ran the restaurant until his death in 1975. His daughter, Kitty Teasley, then took over the restaurant and ran it until 1982. After that, Hartman's building was leased to various people who operated the restaurant under the Hartman's name; however, Hartman's closed for good in 2001.

HARVEY'S CAFETERIA
105 EAST MAIN STREET

After working in the University Dining Room while he was a student at the University of North Carolina in the 1920s, Harvey Rape decided to pursue a career in cafeterias. After college, Rape worked for the S&W Cafeteria chain in Charlotte before he decided to open his own restaurant. He chose Durham as its site and opened Harvey's Cafeteria in 1936. The venture proved to be successful, and the cafeteria became a popular dining spot for downtown workers and was often used as a venue for meetings. Rape even doubled the size of his establishment and took over the site of Markham's Clothing Store next door after the war.

The serving line at Harvey's Cafeteria in 1955. *Photo by Charles Cooper. Courtesy of the Durham Herald Collection, University of North Carolina–Chapel Hill.*

Chef John Singletary and his staff at work in the kitchen at Harvey's Cafeteria. Harvey Rape may be known for his opposition to desegregation, but ironically, his African American kitchen staff was responsible for much of the cafeteria's success. *Photo by Charles Cooper. Courtesy of the Durham Herald Collection, University of North Carolina–Chapel Hill.*

In 1951, according to *Durham and Her People*, Harvey's Cafeteria had a main dining room downstairs that sat 200 people, and it had an additional dining room upstairs. The cafeteria also had a main banquet hall that could accommodate 175 people, and it had three smaller event rooms. Harvey's closed in 1967, and the building that housed it was torn down to make way for Duke Power's new headquarters.

HONEY'S
2702 GUESS ROAD

For twenty-four hours a day, every day (excluding Christmas), the neon sign in front of Honey's welcomed Durham diners for over five decades. With a special of honey-dipped fried chicken and a menu of home-style Southern favorites, including mac and cheese and turnip greens, Honey's

The interior of Honey's, complete with phones for the guests to summon the waitstaff, in 1962. *Courtesy of the Roland Giduz Photographic Collection, University of North Carolina–Chapel Hill.*

served multiple generations of families, interstate travelers and local college students who were seeking late-night sustenance.

Honey's actually began as part of a Charlotte-based chain owned by entrepreneur Y.L. Honey. Beginning with an ice cream stand in Thomasville in 1930, Honey operated several businesses throughout the Carolinas. One of those ventures, the Minute Grill in Charlotte, was eventually renamed for its owner in the 1950s. It became the flagship restaurant of a regional chain that eventually had locations in Greensboro, Chapel Hill and several other North Carolina towns. Over time, the other locations closed and left the Durham restaurant, which opened in 1961, as the last remaining Honey's. It was eventually sold to long-time employee Buck Dickerson, who licensed the name from the Honey family and ran the restaurant from 2005 to 2013. However, Honey's neon sign went dark for good in August 2013, when the lease on the land expired and the owners of the property announced that they had other plans for it. The site, which is just off I-85's exit 175, is now the location of a McDonald's franchise.

Honey's brings back great memories of college and being a young professional. Several of us girls would go to a dance club in Durham called Blue Chips, and Honey's was our late-night snack place with some of our guy friends. We often would stay there until [it was] almost time for the sun to come up, eating and laughing. The food was your typical diner fare, but it was very good, and there was always a crowd there. I even took my parents there a few times when they visited, because the food was that good.
—*Michelle Cobb*

Back in the late 1990s, I worked for a now-defunct video store on Hillsborough Road. After closing, our group would often all go to the Green Room and shoot pool until the wee hours. The only spot to get something to eat after our pool hall shenanigans was Honey's. It was a destination for many [of our] late-night, deep discussions or just bull shooting. That time in my life was one where I felt so profoundly supported and understood by so many vastly different personalities. We were a crazy hodgepodge of characters, and we pulled together, often at Honey's, to be each other's safe place for a while. I think about those guys often, and while I know where a couple landed in life, others have slipped away. Who knew biscuits and gravy could be so therapeutic! I remember being so sad when I drove by after they had bulldozed the place.
—*Christa Slaughter*

THE IVY ROOM
1000 WEST MAIN STREET

One of the city's most beloved dining establishments, the Ivy Room, remained a popular dining destination for Duke students and town residents alike for forty years. Founded in 1945 by Percy Poole, the Ivy Room was essentially a combination of many things. Sporting the slogan "A bit of New York," the restaurant had a deli component that sold food and beverages

The dining room of the Ivy Room. *Courtesy of the Roland Giduz Photographic Collection, University of North Carolina–Chapel Hill.*

that were uncommon in North Carolina. According to *Bull on Bull: Duke's Guide to Durham* in 1982, "Whether you're craving a full southern meal or just a bite from its [New York–style] deli, the Ivy Room has the victuals that will hit the spot."

Upstairs from the Ivy Room's deli was the restaurant's Cosmopolitan Tap Room, a bar that was well-known for its beer selection. Additionally, the Ivy Room was a licensed server of Chicken in the Rough, a brand invented by Oklahoma City restaurateur Beverly Osborne and his wife, Rubye, in 1936. The dish, which consisted of half a fried chicken, shoe-string potatoes and a biscuit with honey, was sold at about 250 different franchise outlets around the country. Chicken in the Rough, which at one

Owner Percy Poole in the gift shop section of the Ivy Room in 1961. *Courtesy of the Roland Giduz Photographic Collection, University of North Carolina–Chapel Hill.*

time rivaled Kentucky Fried Chicken in the fried chicken market, was highly branded. Everything, from dishes to napkins, had the Chicken in the Rough logo on it. The Ivy Room even had a sign hanging in front of the restaurant that featured the official logo: a cigar-smoking rooster brandishing a broken golf club. Chicken in the Rough was popular with students, and the Ivy Room regularly advertised it in the *Duke Chronicle*. In the mid-1960s, on "Student Night" (Wednesdays), Chicken in the Rough was even offered for $1.09 instead of the usual $1.35.

The Ivy Room, which had the motto "It's fun to be nice to people," was also famous for the carton caricatures of its regular customers and waitstaff that hung on the walls. Some waitresses worked there for years, and the most notable of them was Freda Gowan. Originally from England, her beehive hairdo and liberal application of makeup made her something of a local celebrity for twenty-seven years. When Gowan died in 2005, the *Durham Herald* even ran an article in tribute to her.

Percy Poole sold the Ivy Room in 1972, and after trading hands between a couple of short-term owners, the restaurant was purchased by Jerry Bleau in 1977. Citing an increase in rent and expensive renovations that were required to be done to the old building by the health department, Bleau decided to close the restaurant. Its last day of business was May 19, 1985.

I loved the Ivy Room. It was nothing fancy. The waitresses were famous, everyone was "Baby" or "Honey." And that gift shop downstairs—they had every brand of cigarette out there for sale. The first time I ever tried French Gauloises, they came from there, but I liked the cigarettes made in Durham better.

—Mel Melton

KING'S SANDWICH SHOP
701 FOSTER STREET

King's is now a Durham institution, but for years, it was just a little takeout lunch place beyond center field of the Durham Athletic Park; it quietly served hotdogs, burgers and sandwiches to local workers.

King's originally opened in 1942 as a small hotdog stand across the street from its current location, but it was forced to move a few years later when the original location was hit by a car and destroyed. A new home was constructed, and in it, King's continued as it had before, while the city changed around it. In 2007, however, the High family, who owned and operated King's, decided to close the restaurant, and the small cinderblock building on the corner of Foster and Geer Streets was left vacant. Three years later, T.J. McDermott saw a chance to resurrect a bit of Durham history; he purchased the building and reopened King's in the summer of 2010.

King's has survived the revitalization of the area around it. Businesses and people have returned to the once-decaying area and—as can be seen by the line that sometimes forms at the walk-up window—King's hotdogs and burgers are more popular now than ever.

LEO'S SEAFOOD
902 NORTH ALSTON AVENUE

Located on the corner of Liberty Street and Angier Avenue, Leo's Seafood was opened in a former laundromat in 1977. Its first owner only lasted six months before selling the restaurant to Donald "Leo" Coates and his wife, Dudley. The Coates' business started out as nothing more than a seafood market for several of Durham's restaurants, including Bullock's Barbecue, and neighborhood retail customers. In 1996, Leo's lost power during Hurricane Fran, and the market was left with a lot of fish on melting ice; so, the Coates decided to cook all of their stock on outdoor cookers before giving it away. This inspired the idea for a restaurant, and before long, a part of Leo's building was converted into a restaurant, where customers could get takeout plates. All types of fried fish and shrimp were offered daily, along with sides like slaw, fried okra, potato salad and the requisite hushpuppies.

Like other small, long-time establishments, Leo's was successful because it found its niche in the community; it offered friendly service and consistently good food. In 2014, Leo's was on the path of a planned expansion to Alston Avenue. The Coates sold the property to the state and decided to retire.

> *Leo's was a staple in the Northeast Central Durham community, and no Friday night was complete unless a trip was made there for fresh croakers or trout. Leo's seemed to have the right corner, the staff was great, and it was always busy as I recall. Leo was down-to-earth and was able to move back and forth, from the restaurant and takeout side to the fresh fish side, where you could pick out the fish that you wanted.*
>
> —*Andre Vann*

LEWIS CAFÉ
807 WEST MAIN STREET

Many small restaurants survived in Durham by drawing in workers from nearby businesses, and Lewis Café was a prime example of this. After the café was opened in 1939 by Lewis Utley, it served a large breakfast and lunchtime crowd that mainly consisted of workers from the Liggett & Myers plant and other surrounding workplaces.

The café was initially located in a converted boxcar that held five stools and three booths, but a new building was built in the late 1940s that provided seating for fifty-six guests. Utley manned the grill and ran the business for twenty-seven years, and his wife, Ruth, usually ran the cash register. When Utley sold the restaurant to Wallace Pickett in 1967, he stayed on as a part-time cook. In 1981, however, the tobacco companies were dying out and left Lewis's without the clientele that had kept it thriving. In addition to Lewis's

The final days of Lewis Café, with Lewis Utley at the grill and Wallace Picket waiting to plate the order. *Photo by Jim Sparks. Courtesy of the Durham Herald Collection, University of North Carolina–Chapel Hill.*

shrinking consumer base, Brightleaf Square was being renovated next door, and the owners needed a parking lot. Picket sold the building to them, and Lewis's served its last breakfast at the end of August 1981.

LIBBY'S TOO
4910 HILLSBOROUGH ROAD

Libby Green started her restaurant career in the early 1970s, when she became a waitress at Big Tub, a meat-and-three café located at 2022 Angier Avenue. Green purchased that restaurant in 1982 and renamed it Libby's. In 1993, she expanded and opened a second location on Hillsborough Road in West Durham, near the Orange County line. Green closed the original Libby's in 1995, but Libby's Too has remained a popular cash-only neighborhood eatery, serving southern staples on Styrofoam plates. The small building is easy to miss; but Monday through Friday, during breakfast and lunch, the parking lot is usually filled with work trucks and the café's nine tables are occupied by diners, many of them regulars.

LITTLE ACORN
706 RIGSBEE AVENUE

While the Ivy Room may have been the favorite for Duke students for more than thirty years, its contemporary, the Little Acorn, was the favorite for many town residents. The nearby tobacco market also brought in many of the Little Acorn's customers.

In 1940, Robert Roycroft and his wife, Virginia, opened what would become one of Durham's most beloved eating establishments: Little Acorn. The restaurant served traditional barbecue, Brunswick stew and fried chicken—nothing out of the ordinary—but the quality of the food, the atmosphere and the location made Little Acorn a success. The restaurant offered private rooms for banquets and small gatherings, and a 1951 write-up in *Durham and Her People* stated that it was "one of the most modernly equipped establishments of its kind in Durham."

Robert Roycroft retired and closed the restaurant in 1971. His son, Earl, continued the family tradition of working in the restaurant business and opened Acorn Family Restaurant at 3311 Guess Road in the late 1970s. It lasted for several years but never gained the following that Little Acorn had.

My family was middle-class; we weren't going to restaurants a lot. So, Little Acorn was the place we went to for barbecue and stew. We typically went on Sunday, and we never went to any other real restaurants. Our idea was that the Little Acorn was a big deal.

—Mike Knowles

Little Acorn restaurant was a highlight for rural children and their families while they were attending 4-H shows and showing their steers and pigs at the warehouse up the street. For many, it was the only sit-down restaurant they ever got to go to! As a young girl, one of my favorite things to do was go to the Little Acorn with my family. I can still remember the barbecue and hushpuppies. We went there for "supper," as dinner was celebrated at lunch for farm families. Also, going shopping in downtown Durham while we were there for the two-day event was a highlight for us from Hillsborough!

—Rachel Hawkins

My mom, Hazel Pollard, was a waitress at the Little Acorn in the early 1950s. Sometimes, when dad went to pick her up, I would go and sit upstairs and eat the ice cream that Mr. Roycroft had given to me. Sometimes,

The sign in front of Little Acorn in 1960. *Courtesy of the Roland Giduz Photographic Collection, University of North Carolina–Chapel Hill.*

A full parking lot at Little Acorn. *Courtesy of the Roland Giduz Photographic Collection, University of North Carolina–Chapel Hill.*

I'd go out back and visit with Tom. He was the cook that cooked the pig over coals and made the place famous. I loved to sit on the end of a piece of wood and chat with him. Tom was never inside and was always out running the cooker for barbecue.

—*Wanda Walton*

MAGNOLIA GRILL
1002 NINTH STREET

It is difficult to calculate the impact that Magnolia Grill had on Durham. Not only was it a ground-breaking restaurant that helped lead a culinary renaissance, but it brought national attention to the city as a whole. It was a place where anniversaries were celebrated, important business dinners were held, and it was a destination for the out-of-town parents of Duke students. Magnolia Grill was also the place where food lovers went to discover new dishes that would expand their gastronomic horizons.

The chefs and owners behind Magnolia Grill were Ben and Karen Barker. Ben Barker, a native of Chapel Hill, attended the Culinary Institute of America in New York. There, he met his wife, Karen, a fellow culinary student. After graduation, the couple returned to North Carolina and worked together at two of the top restaurants in the state at that time: La Residence and, later, Fearrington House. In 1986, the Barkers took a chance on Durham and decided to open Magnolia Grill. They chose to locate their restaurant in a 1940s building that had originally housed Scarboro's Food Store and later, beginning in 1981, Wellspring Grocery. In 1985, Wellspring had moved to a larger space down the street, so the building was available.

At Magnolia, the Barkers began to create a reinterpretation of Southern cuisine. The city and, indeed, most of the South had not seen anything like the recipes that were being served in Durham. Fame soon followed, and before long, Magnolia Grill was attracting attention from publications, including *Bon Appetit*, *Food & Wine*, the *New York Times* and *Southern Living*. The list of the restaurant's awards also grew. After being a finalist for the "Best Chef in the South" award several times in the 1990s, Ben Barker took home the award from the James Beard Foundation in 2000. Three years later, Karen Barker won her own James Beard Award in the best pastry chef category. *Gourmet* magazine even ranked Magnolia Grill in eleventh

Magnolia Grill in 1989. *Photo by Harold Moore. Courtesy of the Durham Herald Collection, University of North Carolina–Chapel Hill.*

place for "America's Best 50 Restaurants." The restaurant's success even resulted in two cookbooks: *Not Afraid of Flavor: Recipes from Magnolia Grill* (2000) and *Sweet Stuff: Karen Barker's American Desserts* (2004).

Aside from the fame that the restaurant achieved, the other big contribution that Magnolia Grill made to the local restaurant scene was the number of quality chefs it produced. So many that were trained there went on to open their own restaurants or work in other acclaimed establishments; among them are Scott Howell, who opened Nana's among others; and Walter Royal, who went on to win on the television show *Iron Chef America* and was named executive chef at Raleigh's famed Angus Barn. Others include Billy and Kelli Cotter, who own the Durham restaurants Dashi and Toast; pastry chef Phoebe Lawless of popular Durham bakery Scratch; Glenn Lozuke of Weaver Street Market; Amanda Orser of Littler in Durham; and may more. The culinary influence that Magnolia Grill has had on Durham and beyond continues to this day.

In 2012, in a move that saddened many Durhamites, the Barkers decided to close Magnolia. Their retirement didn't last long, however, and the Barkers helped their son, Gabe, open Carrboro's acclaimed Pizzeria

Mercato in 2016. As for the former home of Magnolia Grill, it was taken over by Monuts, a popular bakery and café.

> *I still remember the rosemary ice cream at Magnolia Grill....And it was amazing to watch all of the chefs come out of there to start their own restaurants.*
>
> —*Mike Howell*

NANA'S
2514 UNIVERSITY DRIVE

Among the people who have had the greatest impact on Durham's restaurant scene, Scott Howell might be at the top. A native of Asheville, Howell trained at the Culinary Institute of America in New York. He went on to work at several restaurants in that city before spending a year at one of the top dining establishments in the world: Italy's San Domenico. In 1990, Howell returned to North Carolina and worked for the Barkers at Magnolia Grill before he decided to open his own restaurant in 1992. Thus, Nana's was born, and the chef whom *Food & Wine* magazine called "a man of formidable talent" began to make his own mark on Durham.

With an extremely creative menu and a wine list that won the prestigious *Wine Spectator* Award of Excellence, Nana's soon brought national attention to Durham. The list of Nana's awards and recognitions is long, and Howell himself is an eight-time James Beard Award semifinalist. The restaurant had few rivals in the city—and even the state—as a destination for celebrations and special nights out.

Nana's went through several changes over the years and was remodeled and expanded in 2000. In June 2018, Howell announced that he was shutting the restaurant's doors. After nine months of being closed, however, he decided to reopen his famed establishment. Nana's easily reclaimed its place as a leader in Durham's fine dining industry.

Scott Howell's effects on Durham dining are not just limited to Nana's. After his restaurant's success, Howell invested in other ventures in Durham, including the Q Shack, NanaSteak, Bar Virgile, NanaTaco and DeeLuxe Chicken. Howell has since sold some of these restaurants, but he constantly comes up with new ideas and has remained at the forefront of dining in Durham.

NINTH STREET BAKERY
136 EAST CHAPEL HILL STREET

As its name implies, Ninth Street Bakery, is, first and foremost, a bakery—its breads and pastries are distributed between Raleigh and Greensboro—but for much of its existence, its restaurant has been an important part of the business.

In the spring of 1981, Ninth Street Bakery opened at 743 Ninth Street (the current location of Dain's) as a retail bakery and a small café. Its founders were brothers George and Frank Ferrell; Maureen Ferrell, Frank's wife; and Michael Mooney, Maureen's brother. The business flourished in its early years—thanks to its delicious baked goods and the public's increasing interest in cafés that focused on healthier and more organic offerings. By 1989, the bakery had outgrown its original location and moved to a larger spot just a block north (the current site of Elmo's). With room to expand, the café part of the business grew into a full-scale restaurant that served everything from coffee and breakfast pastries to dinner entrées and desserts.

A group in front of the original Ninth Street bakery location in 1989. Radio host Bob Burtman is on the left, and next to him is John Valentine, the co-founder and owner of Durham's legendary Regulator Bookshop for forty years. *Photo by Harold Moore. Courtesy of the Durham Herald Collection, University of North Carolina–Chapel Hill.*

In 1992, as the restaurant part of the business continued to increase in popularity and the demand for bread products grew, Ninth Street's bakery operations moved downtown to the current location of Ninth Street Bakery. Four years later, the owners decided to turn their focus back to the bakery part of the business and closed the restaurant.

Though it is primarily a wholesale operation, the downtown location did have a small, retail take-out counter for coffee and pastries. Over time, it grew into a true lunch café, with seating and a much-expanded menu. In the fall of 2013, the original owners decided to retire and sold Ninth Street Bakery to Ari Berenbaum, one of their former bakers. Berenbaum has continued to run the business and kept Ninth Street Bakery at the forefront of Durham's food scene.

THE ORIENTAL
116 EAST PARRISH STREET

Chinese cuisine was about as exotic as food got in Durham when the Oriental opened in 1938. It was, most likely, only the second restaurant in the state to serve any kind of Asian cuisine (a restaurant of the same name—apparently not connected—opened in Charlotte in the 1920s).

The Oriental was founded by Wo Der, and the 1948 Durham city guide listed Paul D. Yuen as a partner. Like many restaurants, the Oriental was run as a family business. When Wo Der died in 1953, his son, Chuck, took over as the manager. The 1959 Durham city guide listed the restaurant's staff as Chuck Yee Der, manager; Jimmie Der, cook; Mrs. W.O. Der.; Lee T. Lung, cook; and Yuen Der Shee, cook.

Manager Chuck Der checks on his kitchen staff at the Oriental in 1954. *Photo by Charles Cooper. Courtesy of the Durham Herald Collection, University of North Carolina– Chapel Hill.*

Though it is largely forgotten today, the Oriental was important to Durham's food history, because it offered Durhamites the chance to step outside of their comfortable worlds of traditional Southern fare. But, for those who were not quite sure about trying Chinese food, the restaurant did advertise that it also offered American food. And, to make diners (who were likely all non-Asian, as there were so few Asians in the city at the time) comfortable, the wait staff consisted of only Caucasian women. After spending thirty years in business, the Oriental closed in 1968.

THE PALACE INTERNATIONAL
1104 A BROAD STREET

Maurice and Caren Ochola, both natives of Kenya, came to the United States to attend American universities. They eventually settled in Durham, where they decided to open a restaurant. The Ocholas chose to focus on African cuisine, because it was the food they knew, and no one else was serving African food in the city. The couple opened the Palace International on Parrish Street in 1989.

In 2001, a serious fire caused the Palace to close, and it appeared to many Durhamites that the restaurant was gone for good; but in 2007, the Ocholas decided to reopen. The pair found a location for their restaurant on Broad Street, which was formerly a florist's shop, and they brought in their son, Moses, and daughter, Suzanna, to run the new restaurant with them. Today, the small restaurant with spartan décor serves as a gathering place for different groups and cultures, and it often features music. The Palace's official website describes its menu as including "both traditional East African delicacies as well as African spins on world cuisines."

THE PALMS RESTAURANT
305 EAST CHAPEL HILL STREET

For over forty years, the Palms was the place where lawyers, judges and downtown businessmen grabbed lunch. Located across the street from the original Washington Duke Hotel—the city's finest—the Palms was also undoubtedly the place where many business deals were made. The

Left: The Palms may be long gone, but its name can still be found in the threshold of the building it once occupied. *Photo by Chris Holaday.*

Below: An advertisement for the Palms from *Hill's 1947 Durham City Directory. Courtesy of Digital NC.*

THE PALMS RESTAURANT

AIR CONDITIONED

305 E. Chapel Hill St.   Opposite Washington Duke Hotel

GOOD FOOD – POPULAR PRICES
PLUS GOOD SERVICE
HOME OF SIZZLING STEAKS

Banquet Hall — Private Dining Room

N. O. REEVES, Prop.   Telephone L-8021

restaurant's banquet room was the site of meetings for many civic groups, and it even hosted events like the 1947 reunion for veterans of the Spanish-American War.

The Palms was opened in 1932 by Richard Green in a building that had previously housed the Liberty Café. Within a few years, however, Green sold the business to Norman Reeves, the proprietor of Reeves's American Inn at 117 East Chapel Hill Street, where a plate lunch cost fifty cents and "coffee was served with pure cream." The Palms' location down the street was better, and it gave Reeves more room, so he closed the American Inn to focus on The Palms.

In 1948, Reeves sold the restaurant to brothers-in-law Otis Capsalis and Michael Vassiliades. Their combined families ran the Palms until 1975, when it was sold to George Kappas and Andrew Katsigiannis. By then, however, Durham's downtown area was dying; the Washington Duke Hotel had been demolished, and businesses were leaving. Even without much competition in the neighborhood, the Palms only made it to 1983 before closing.

PARIZÄDE
2200 WEST MAIN STREET

The story of Parizäde cannot be told without first telling the story of Giorgios Bakatsias. As a native of Greece who came to the United States with his family at the age of twelve, Bakatsias opened his first restaurant in North Carolina when he was in his early twenties. By the 1980s, he was firmly on his way to becoming one of North Carolina's top restaurateurs. Bakatsias's influence in the restaurant world is undeniable, and in 2014, he was a finalist for the James Beard Foundation's award in the outstanding restaurateur category. His innovative restaurants can be found in Chapel Hill and Raleigh, but Durham is where it all began.

In 1990, Bakatsias opened Parizäde, which is considered by many to be the crown jewel of his restaurant empire. Parizäde is located on the ground floor of the Erwin Square office building, which was once the site of Erwin Textile Mill; its nondescript exterior belies what is inside. According to *Southern Living* magazine, "The doors open into a fantasy world, the menu

Giorgios Bakatsias inside Taverna Nikos, one of his other Durham creations, in 1989. *Photo by Jim Sparks. Courtesy of the Durham Herald Collection, University of North Carolina–Chapel Hill.*

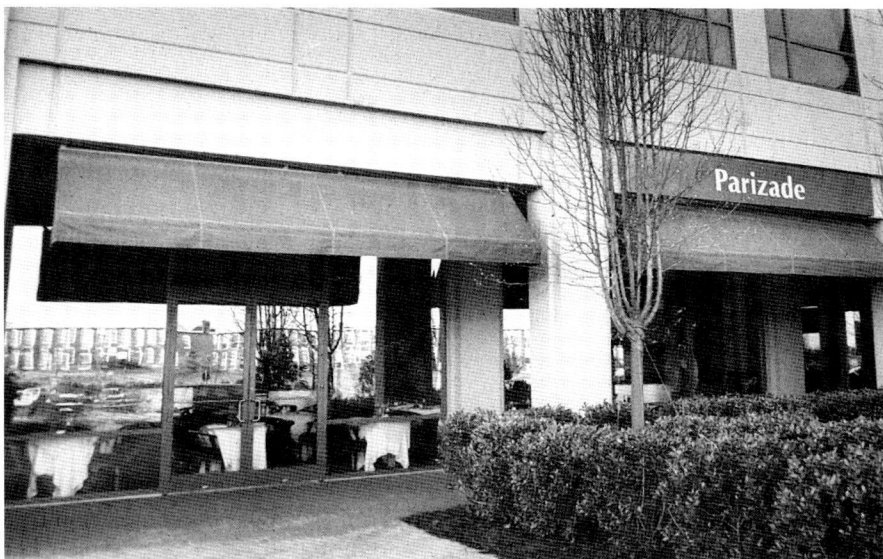

The exterior of Parizäde, which was located on the bottom floor of the Erwin Square office building, gave little indication to the elaborate décor and famed cuisine diners could find inside. *Courtesy of the Durham Herald Collection, University of North Carolina–Chapel Hill.*

whirls you through the Mediterranean. The ebullient atmosphere reflects the personality of longtime Durham restaurateur Giorgios Bakatsias."

Not all of Bakatsias's creations have proven to be successful, but several in Durham, including Parizäde, have played an important role in developing the city's food scene. Among Bakatsias's successes are George's Garage on Ninth Street, which closed in 2009 after fifteen years; and Bakatsias's Cuisine on Hillandale in Loehman's Plaza, which opened in 1981 and closed in 2003. Among his current Durham restaurants are Vin Rouge, a French bistro at the intersection of Hillsborough and Ninth Streets; and the critically acclaimed café at Duke's Nasher Museum of Art.

> *Parizäde has always been one of my favorite restaurants in Durham, particularly for special occasions. I remember two friends and I going there for a birthday celebration; we got all dressed up and enjoyed ourselves with what we considered a fancy meal. The calamari were to die for…not sure there's been another restaurant to beat it. We had it all—the appetizer, wine, meal and dessert!*
>
> —*Michelle Cobb*

PARKER'S
706 EAST MAIN STREET

In 1958, former cab driver Hugh Parker and his wife, Edith, opened Parker's restaurant. With a rotating menu of meats and vegetables, the diner filled its counter and booths with customers for over thirty years. Although Parker's started with a clientele primarily consisting of mill workers from East Durham, it quickly became a favorite of Duke students. The restaurant's good, home-style cooking and Hugh Parker's gracious hospitality made Parker's a Duke institution for two generations, despite the fact that it was located across town from Duke's campus. According to the *Duke Chronicle*, "Parker's is a place where southerners and non-southerners alike can experience delicious homemade southern cooking in a real, down home atmosphere." Sadly, Parker's closed in 1992.

Though Parker's building is surrounded by development today, it is still home to a restaurant. With the memorable motto, "Where the food is anointed and you won't be disappointed," JC's Kitchen is famous in its own right. Founded by Shelah Lee and taken over by her sister, Phyllis Terry, in 2008, JC's has been serving soul food since 1998.

One time at Parker's, I order a fried chicken sandwich. When it came, it was a big piece of fried chicken—bones and all—between two pieces of bread. It took a little bit of work, but it was delicious.

—*Bob Burtman*

PIPER'S DELI
3219 OLD CHAPEL HILL ROAD

In 1984, Piper Lunsford and her father, Wendell, opened Piper's Deli. With no pretense, the deli was a neighborhood restaurant that focused on serving good burgers and sandwiches. It soon developed a loyal following, particularly with the lunch crowd.

The Lunsfords sold the restaurant in 1998, but it retained the original name and concept. In June 2019, Piper's announced that it was closing at the end of the month and reopening with a new name after the July Fourth weekend; it reopened as Steel Spatula Burger Company.

Piper's Deli in 1990. *Photo by Jim Sparks. Courtesy of the Durham Herald Collection, University of North Carolina–Chapel Hill.*

Piper Lunsford went on to partner with Wendy Woods and opened Piper's in the Park on South Miami Boulevard in 1999. The pair then opened a popular breakfast spot called NOSH at 2812 Erwin Road in 2006.

PIZZA PALACE
2002 HILLSBOROUGH ROAD

Pizza Palace, likely only the second place in Durham to specialize in pizza, opened in 1965 on the corner of Ninth Street and Hillsborough Road by Jimmy Renn. It soon became a popular destination for good pizza and cheap beer, and it was especially popular with students.

In 1978, accountant Harry Rodenhizer bought the restaurant. He later served two terms as mayor, from 1979 to 1981, and from 1991 to 1993. During his second term, Rodenhizer helped put together a financial package to persuade the owner of the Durham Bulls to keep the team in Durham. The new stadium that was built as a result—Durham Bulls Athletic Park—helped spur new development in downtown Durham and the eventual opening of many new restaurants.

Harry Rodenhizer's daughter, Faye, took over Pizza Palace in 2002. She oversaw its relocation from Ninth Street to Guess Road in 2004. However, the restaurant was closed for good on the last day of 2008. The Pizza Palace's original site became home to Giorgios Bakatsias's short-lived Grasshopper Asian Kitchen, which was replaced by Chef Tim Lyons's Blu Seafood and Bar, which opened in 2007 and closed in 2019.

> *Way down Guess Road, past Granny's Panties, sat Pizza Palace. In a building that looked like a cross between a new age church and castle, Pizza Palace offered somewhat forgettable Italian food in a place that led to some of my favorite Durham dining memories. Karaoke on Thursday nights with an average age of seventy-five, lovable barflies watching basketball in the upstairs bar…Pizza Palace always felt like a place where you may not find the best food in town, but you'd walk away with a story.*
>
> —*Chris Reid*

PULCINELLA'S
4711 HOPE VALLEY ROAD

A casual neighborhood Italian restaurant is an essential part of many cities' dining scenes. In the Hope Valley and Woodcroft areas of Durham, that niche is filled by Pulcinella's. A classic, red-sauce establishment that has served the cuisine of southern Italy since 1994, Pulcinella's is named after the comedic character of the same name that represents Naples and its lifestyle (he is well known for his white costume and simple black mask, as evidenced by the many images of him in the restaurant).

The personalities of Pulcinella's owners, Salvatore "Rino" Fevola (who passed away in 2019) and Mike Hassan, have always been a big part of the restaurant's success. They frequently greeted guests—many of them regulars returning for the welcoming atmosphere, friendly service and consistently good pizza and pasta dishes that can be found at Pulcinella's.

SADDLE CLUB AKA SADDLE AND FOX
3211 HILLSBOROUGH ROAD

For nearly forty years, Saddle and Fox was Durham's "fancy steakhouse." It was a place for special celebrations, prom nights, graduations, fraternity events, and it was a destination for Duke alumni returning for a football game on the weekends.

Charles "Sonny" Haynes graduated from Durham High School and attended Duke, where he played football. Afterward, he joined the military, and it was while he was serving in Europe during World War II that he discovered his passion for food. Haynes returned from military service, and in 1946, he built the Saddle Club restaurant on land that had been the location of his family's horse stables and riding school.

With a large stove fireplace, wagon wheels on the wall and horse-themed décor, the restaurant was built with a rustic atmosphere. Haynes developed a French-themed menu and even offered what was a reportedly the first salad bar in Durham. Live bands and piano players frequently entertained diners, while the jukebox was popular in the bar. In front of the restaurant, there was a huge mound of shells from the restaurant's oyster bar, and it

The Saddle and Fox in the 1960s, complete with an oyster shell mound. *Courtesy of the Charles C. Haynes Papers, University of North Carolina–Chapel Hill.*

Inside the Saddle and Fox in the 1970s. *Photo by Jim Thornton. Courtesy of the Durham Herald Collection, University of North Carolina–Chapel Hill.*

became something of a testament to its success. Haynes was ever-present in the restaurant, as was his wife, Ruby, who served as hostess, and Walter Grandy, who was the restaurant's maître d' for over thirty years.

In the late 1940s and early 1950s, photos of the restaurant filled with Duke students frequently appeared in the *Chanticleer*, the university's yearbook. The 1952 edition even captioned a photo of dancing students: "Favorite haunt of Dukesters seeking escape from Gothic and Georgian atmosphere is the crowded Saddle Club. Couples sway to the jukebox's tunes." In its later years, the Saddle and Fox entertained an older crowd, but Haynes maintained a connection to his alma mater; in 1982, Duke's guide to the city that it issued for students stated, "Let Mom and Dad take you to an old-time Duke standard."

In the mid-1980s, Haynes retired and sold the Saddle and Fox. The large space was then divided into two restaurants: Cattleman's Steak House and Italian Garden. They both closed in 2009 and were replaced by an auto parts store.

SALADELIA CAFÉ
4201 UNIVERSITY DRIVE #101

Since 1988, Saladelia has been serving a combination of Lebanese and Greek cuisine in a strip mall on University Drive. Its wide assortment of fresh Mediterranean fare (not to mention its famous baklava) has been so popular that its owners, Robert and Fida Ghanem, have had to expand the original location twice. They have also added other locations around the Triangle, including one on Duke's campus and another at American Tobacco.

In 2008, the Ghanems purchased the popular Mad Hatter's Café and Bakeshop from its original owners, Grace Nordhoff and Jason Balius. In a location that is across the street from Duke's East Campus, Mad Hatter's has been a Durham institution in its own right since the late 1990s.

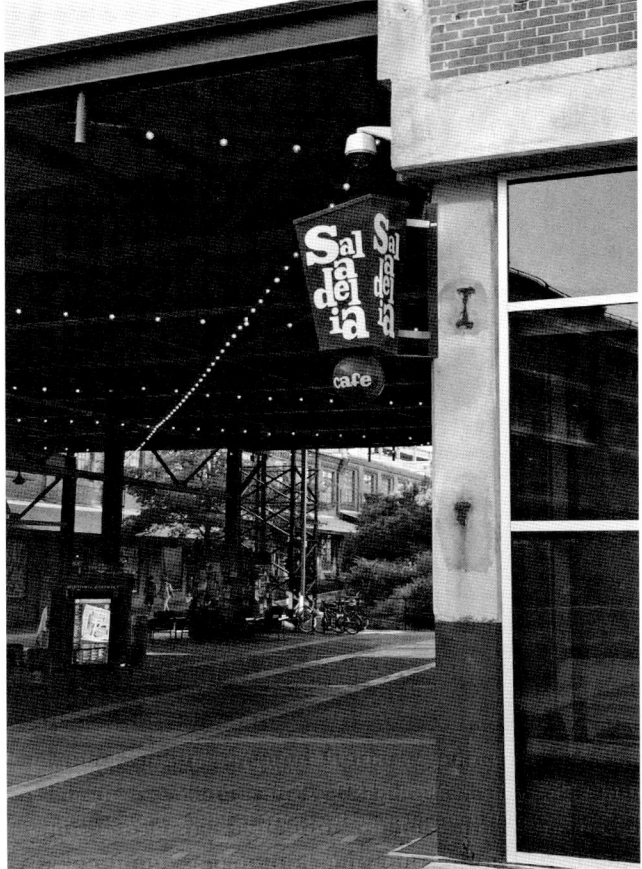

Saladelia Café, a popular lunch destination for those who worked in the repurposed American Tobacco campus for over a decade, opened in the lobby of the Crowe Building in 2008. *Photo by Chris Holaday.*

SATISFACTION
LAKEWOOD SHOPPING CENTER, BRIGHTLEAF SQUARE

Pizza, beer and televised sports are how diners (and imbibers) have summed up their visits to Satisfaction for over thirty years. When Satisfaction opened in 1982 in Lakewood Shopping Center, it was promoted as a destination for pizza, subs, a full bar and video games. It soon became popular with Duke students, and early ads even proclaimed that it was "Duke's Bar." The establishment apparently even attracted attention outside of Durham, as a 1987 advertisement in the *Duke Chronicle* featured a quote that had appeared in *Rolling Stone* magazine. It stated, "Satisfaction fulfills that ultimate student-hangout criterion: running into friends and talking loudly over loud music."

In 1993, Satisfaction moved to a large space at Brightleaf Square. There, fans and families alike enjoyed pizza and beer in a casual atmosphere (the décor even included half of a Volkswagen Beetle) for twenty-five years. It was then purchased by Staton Ellis in 2004, and as times changed and dining options increased, crowds would only visit the once-busy restaurant to watch big sporting events. This was not enough to maintain the business, and Ellis decided to close the Durham institution in the summer of 2018.

SHANGHAI
3433 HILLSBOROUGH ROAD

In a strip mall that has seen numerous tenants come and go, Shanghai has remained the one constant. It opened in the early 1980s and has consistently remained one of Durham's most popular Chinese restaurants. It is always busy at lunchtime, and takeout orders are often lined up in bags on the counter. Diners are always treated to a pot of green tea when they are seated—a tradition that makes the restaurant unique.

In the early 2000s, the restaurant was purchased by Chef Ah Lack Wong and his wife, Lilly. The restaurant offers Americanized Chinese food, but its specialty is Cantonese cuisine. Many Durhamites visit Shanghai for its authentic dishes from that region.

SHRIMP BOATS
2637 CHAPEL HILL BOULEVARD

Chain restaurants certainly have an important place in American restaurant history, but we have tried to stay away from them in this book because they are not unique to Durham. One exception to this, however, is Shrimp Boats, which was located on Chapel Hill Boulevard from 1969 until 2016. Actually, most Durhamites are probably not even aware that it was a chain, since it only had one location in the city. In reality, however,

United States Patent Office

Des. 217,055
Patented Mar. 31, 1970

217,055
CARRY OUT RESTAURANT

Tilmon Chamlee, Macon, Ga., assignor to The Shrimp Boats, Inc., Macon, Ga., a corporation of Georgia

Filed Jan. 27, 1969, Ser. No. 15,517

Term of patent 14 years

Int. Cl. D25—04

U.S. Cl. D13—1

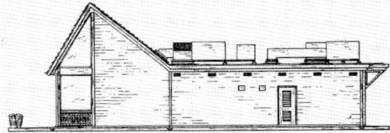

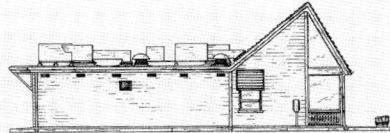

Like some other chains, Shrimp Boats restaurants were located in identical buildings. The design was patented in 1970. *Courtesy of the United States Patent Office.*

Durham's Shrimp Boats location was just one of ninety-fives stores that stretched from Georgia to Virginia.

The Shrimp Boat was founded in Macon, Georgia, in the mid-1950s. In the late 1960s, the company went through a major rebranding, which added the "s" to the name and started its expansion. Through the first part of the 1970s, new Shrimp Boats restaurants were constructed in a uniform style, with steeply pitched roofs and distinctive beams that jutted through the eaves. Durham's Shrimp Boats was opened in 1969 by John Workman. Workman maintained the name and kept the restaurant going independently, even after the chain collapsed in the 1970s. He sold the business in 1997 to two of his employees, Nancy Norwood and her husband, Mohammed Yousef.

Despite its name, the restaurant did not just serve seafood; in fact, it may have been most well known for its fried chicken and traditional southern sides, as well as its motto: "Treasure of Eating Pleasure." Perhaps one of the most notable things about the Durham location of Shrimp Boats is that the building was one of the best-preserved examples of the chain's unique architecture style. Shrimp Boats Durham location finally closed in 2016. In December 2017, Chef Ricky Moore took over the site and opened a second location of his highly-acclaimed Saltbox Seafood Joint.

SPARTACUS
4139 DURHAM–CHAPEL HILL BOULEVARD

There have long been Greek restaurateurs in Durham, but it wasn't until the 1980s that the city's residents were actually ready to eat real Greek cuisine. In 1993, Nondas Kalfas, who came from a long line of restaurateurs, and John Drury opened Spartacus to provide a more casual, family-friendly Greek restaurant. The restaurant's lobby was filled with old family photos, and diners were greeted by the same hostess, Helen Vurnakes, for the entirety of the restaurant's existence. Spartacus soon became famous for its weekend buffets, which were filled with Greek delicacies that gave diners the chance to expand their culinary horizons. When Spartacus closed in the summer of 2016, it left a noticeable void in the city's restaurant offerings.

THE SUB WAY (BULL CITY SUBS)
914 WEST MAIN STREET OR 104 ALBEMARLE STREET

With a large selection of submarine sandwiches as well as beer, the Sub Way became popular with students and downtown workers in the mid-1970s. The fact that it delivered—a rarity at the time—only increased the restaurant's popularity. Diners who were really hungry could even tackle "The Big One," the Sub Way's giant sandwich creation.

The Sub Way's name actually kept the national chain from using the name "Subway" in Durham for several years; the chain's name was even changed to BMT Subway Deli so that it could be separated from the local establishment. In 1988, the chain officially paid the local store to change its name to Bull City Subs. It finally closed in 2003, and another popular dining and drinking spot, the Federal, opened in its location the following year.

> *Taking over the space from Bull City Subs (formerly the Sub Way until the national chain paid them to change their name) was difficult. You could sense the history of the place and what it meant to many a city worker that kept coming by and wondering what was happening. After over twenty years, the "patina" was hard to scrub out of that place! We were lucky to acquire the lease in a building that had so much history. When we pulled the wood away from the front and sides of the building, we saw the history of it as a market and a leather shop.*
> —*Josh Wittman, co-owner of the Federal*

TIP-TOP FISH HOUSE
3300 HILLSBOROUGH ROAD

When Percy and Ione Watkins opened Tip-Top Fish House in the late 1950s, it was a small, sixty-seat establishment on West Hillsborough Road, in the vicinity of what is now the Dog House. Percy Watkins had worked in the grocery business before he ventured into the restaurant world, and in the 1950s, he also became a partner in Burlington and Raleigh restaurants.

In 1960, the Watkinses took on a partner named Norris Lawing, and together, they opened something of a state-of-the-art restaurant just a couple of blocks to the east. Designed by noted modernist architect Frank DePasquale, the Tip-Top Fish House had a unique fish motif and seating for

Above: Tip-Top Fish House was as famous for its seafood as it was for its unique architecture. This ad is from the *1963 Hill's Durham City Directory.*

Left: A 1969 ad for Tip-Top Fish House. *Courtesy of Belinda Watkins Rasmussen.*

over two hundred customers. In addition to seafood, the restaurant served steaks, fried chicken and barbecue, but it was the fried fish and shrimp that kept the establishment popular for so long.

Percy Watkins passed away unexpectedly in 1963, but Ione Watkins and Lawing continued to run the restaurant. The area soon became a dining destination, with Saddle and Fox just down the street and Bullock's—which moved there in 1970—just behind the Fish House. In the mid-1980s, Watkins and Lawing decided to retire and sold the establishment. It remained in business as the Galley for a period of time before it was transformed into a nightclub. The site is now occupied by a Walgreens drugstore.

TURNAGE'S BARBECUE
608 MORRENE ROAD

Before he owned his own restaurant, Josh Turnage worked as a cotton buyer for Erwin Mills and cooked hogs for a hobby. He started his career just cooking for friends, but word about his barbecue spread, and people wanted to buy it. In the late 1930s, he opened a small establishment that was only open one day per week. It grew in popularity, but in 1946, Turnage sold the business to Jim Warren, one of his former cooks. Warren continued using the Turnage name and expanded the restaurant. He continued to serve pit-cooked barbecue, Brunswick stew and the usual assortment of sides for nearly twenty-five years in the restaurant's large rustic building that featured a stone fireplace and pits for cooking the hogs.

TURNAGE'S BARBECUE

"37 Years"

You'll Enjoy Eating Here!

JAMES W. WARREN, Owner

Now Open Tuesday, Thursday and Saturday
FOR THE PUBLIC

Private Parties - Monday - Wednesday - Friday and Sunday

604 Morreene Road   **Call 286-9117**

Turnage's Barbecue ad from Hill's 1963 Durham City Guide. Courtesy of Digital NC.

As shown in this 1955 photograph, Turnage's slow-cooked hogs in the traditional way: over pits filled with coals. *Photo by Harold Moore. Courtesy of the Durham Herald Collection, University of North Carolina–Chapel Hill.*

Located on the western edge of Durham, Turnage's Barbecue drew college students from Duke and the University of North Carolina, and it was frequently the site of fraternity and sorority events for both schools. When the 1942 Rose Bowl was famously played in Durham due to World War II, the visiting Oregon Beavers' football team enjoyed some good North Carolina pork barbecue from Josh Turnage. In the 1950s, university-affiliated jazz bands often entertained the restaurant's diners.

Turnage's was also among the first white-owned restaurants in Durham to desegregate. On May 25, 1963, the black-owned *Carolina Times* announced that seven Durham restaurants were voluntarily desegregating. Turnage's was listed, as were the Blue Light and Tops. Turnage's continued to operate successfully through the 1960s but was closed in 1970, when Warren decided to pursue a new career in the real estate business. Maitland Nance then bought the restaurant's location, where he opened Nance Seafood. The location is now home to a veterinary clinic.

WHIT'S GRILL
748 NINTH STREET

While businesses of all types came and went on Ninth Street, Whit's Grill was a fixture there for over twenty years. With Erwin Mill across the street and Duke's east campus a block to the east, Whit's served a variety of customers; blue-collar workers just off the night shift may have stopped by for breakfast and college students may have gone by looking for a quick lunch. But they all came for Whit's home-style fare, especially its famed plate of smoked sausage links.

The building that housed Whit's Grill was built in the 1920s and had many tenants over the years. The 1956 Durham city guide listed the location as the Whitaker Brothers Grocery and Market. By 1958, however, Everett and Lloyd Whitaker had decided to convert their business to a grill. When Erwin Mill closed, Whit's lost a large part of its customer base, and the restaurant closed in 1980. The building then housed a pizzeria for a time before becoming a Mr. Hoagie sub shop by the early 1990s. Chubby's Tacos later took over the space.

WIMPY'S GRILL
617 HICKS STREET

As a cash-only and takeout-only eatery, Wimpy's Grill had a place in the stomachs of Durhamites for thirty-two years. At breakfast and lunchtime, a crowd of people could normally be found packed into the small interior as they all placed orders at the window and waited for their names to be called.

In 1987, Larry and Brenda Mishoe opened their grill on a Hillsborough Road corner. After a stint in the army as a cook, Larry Mishoe had been working as a butcher at Harris Teeter and Durham's A&P (the location is now occupied by Whole Foods). When Mishoe and his wife opened Wimpy's, he continued grinding his own beef, which may have been a part of Wimpy's success, as its burgers soon made it famous. In 2009, the Travel Channel sent *Man v. Food* host Adam Richman to Durham to tackle Wimpy's garbage burger. He succeeded in eating the giant (and messy) burger, and in the process, he brought national attention to the small eatery. But it wasn't just burgers that kept Wimpy's popular—everything the restaurant served was homemade, from the biscuits and slaw to the banana pudding.

When the Mishoes' employee of twenty-eight years, Sandra Dorman, retired, they soon decided that it was time to follow suit. When they closed Wimpy's in late May 2019, it was actually a day earlier than planned. When word of the closing spread, a rush of patrons came in for a final burger, and they purchased all of the burgers that were available.

YAMAZUSHI
4711 HOPE VALLEY ROAD

In the mid-1980s, most Durhamites probably associated Japanese cuisine with large tabletop grills manned by entertaining chefs. In 1986, however, George and Mayumi Yamazawa opened Yamazushi, a typical sushi bar, in the Woodcroft Shopping Center. Despite the fact that sushi had not yet become a popular mainstream dining option, Yamazushi prevailed and expanded the culinary horizons of many Durham diners along the way. In 2010, the Yamazawas took their Japanese dining experience even further; they changed Yamazushi to a *kaiseki* restaurant. Kaiseki restaurants serve multicourse dinners featuring a variety of small dishes, which are served in a ceremonial fashion. This leisurely dining experience—rare is this country—is only offered to a few patrons per night.

Bibliography

Newspapers and Magazines

Carolina Times
Duke Chronicle
Durham Magazine
Durham Morning Herald (1945–1991)
Durham Sun (1945–1991)
Herald-Sun (1991–Present)
Hill's Durham City Directory
Indy Week
Our State
Southern Living

Books

Anderson, Jean Bradley. *Durham County: A History of Durham County, North Carolina*. Durham, NC: Duke University Press, 1990.

Cohen Ferris, Marcie. *The Edible South: The Power of Food and the Making of an American Region*. Chapel Hill: University of North Carolina Press, 2016.

Dula, W.C., and A.C. Simpson. *Durham and Her People: Combining History and Who's Who in Durham of 1949 and 1950*. Durham, NC: Citizens Press, 1951.

Evans, Eli N. *The Provincials: A Personal History of Jews in the South*. New York: Free Press Paperbacks, 1997.

Massengill, Stephen E. *Durham, North Carolina*. Charleston, SC: Arcadia Publishing, 1997.

Prospero, Ann. *Chefs of the Triangle: Their Lives, Recipes and Restaurants*. Winston-Salem, NC: John F. Blair Publishers, 2009.

Reed, John Shelton, and Dale Volberg Reed. *Holy Smoke, The Big Book of North Carolina Barbecue*. Chapel Hill: University of North Carolina Press, 2008.

Vann, Andre D. *African Americans of Durham County*. Charleston, SC: Arcadia Publishing, 2017.

———. *Durham's Hayti*. Charleston, SC: Arcadia Publishing 1999.

Other Sources

Charles C. Haynes Papers #5398. Southern Historical Collection, Wilson Library, University of North Carolina–Chapel Hill.

Durham Herald Co. Newspaper Photograph Collection #P0105. North Carolina Collection Photographic Archives, Wilson Library, University of North Carolina–Chapel Hill.

Durwood Barbour Collection of North Carolina Postcards #P0077. North Carolina Collection Photographic Archives, Wilson Library, University of North Carolina–Chapel Hill.

Farm Security Administration, Office of War Information Collection, Library of Congress.

Jerome Friar Photographic Collection and Related Materials #P0090. North Carolina Collection Photographic Archives, Wilson Library, University of North Carolina–Chapel Hill.

North Carolina Collection, Durham County Library, Steve Gaddis Photograph Collection.

North Carolina Digital Heritage Center (digitalnc.org)

Roland Giduz Photographic Collection #P0033. North Carolina Collection Photographic Archives, Wilson Library, University of North Carolina–Chapel Hill.

Index

W

Wabash Express Steakhouse 22
Washington Duke Hotel 49, 50, 98
Washington Duke Inn & Golf Club
        9, 53, 77
Watkins, Ione 111
Watkins, Percy 111
Whitaker, Everett 115
Whitaker, Lloyd 115
Whit's Grill 115
Wimpy's Grill 33, 115
Winston, Charles 47
Wittman, Josh 12, 111
Wolcott, Marion Post 27
Wong, Ah Lack 108
Wong, Lilly 108
Woods, Wendy 103

Y

Yamazawa, George 116
Yamazawa, Mayumi 116
Yamazushi 41, 116

About the Authors

Chris Holaday lives in Durham and is the author of a number of books, including *Southern Breads* and several on the topic of baseball. He graduated from the University of North Carolina at Chapel Hill and received a master's degree in history from North Carolina Central University in Durham.

For nearly twenty years, Patrick Cullom has worked to preserve and ensure access to historic photographic materials. Since 2007, he has served as a visual materials processing archivist for the Wilson Special Collections Library at the University of North Carolina at Chapel Hill. Throughout his career as a processing archivist, Cullom has encountered millions of photographic images, each created using a variety of formats, that depict a wide array of subjects. In addition to working at UNC–Chapel Hill, Patrick grew up in Raleigh and is a proud North Carolina State University alumnus. As such, he is especially honored to play a part in preserving and sharing North Carolina's rich photographic history. He currently lives in Raleigh with his family and an assortment of four-legged furry friends.

Visit us at
www.historypress.com